# The Mountain Bike Way of Knowledge

A cartoon self-help manual on riding technique
and general mountain bike craziness....

## William Nealy

MENASHA RIDGE PRESS
Your Guide to the Outdoors Since 1982
an imprint of AdventureKEEN

To my friend
John Dolbeare
1957 – 1989

# The Mountain Bike Way of Knowledge:
# A cartoon self-help manual on riding technique
# and general mountain bike craziness...

Copyright 1989, 1999, and 2023 by William J. Nealy
All rights reserved
Printed in the United States of America

## Published by

**MENASHA RIDGE PRESS**
Your Guide to the Outdoors Since 1982
an imprint of AdventureKEEN

2204 First Ave. S., Ste. 102
Birmingham, Alabama 35233
800-678-7006, FAX 877-374-9016
adventurewithkeen.com

ISBN 978-1-63404-368-7 (pbk); ISBN 978-1-63404-369-4 (ebook)

# PUBLISHER'S NOTE

What you hold in your hands is a book of William Nealy's art, pulled from the gnarliest Class VI rapids of time . . . almost lost forever.

But now Nealy's zany illustrations have been bound and bandaged together in a new monumental collection, including books and cartoons long out of print. Nealy's full-speed downhill no-holds-barred art has been reset and brought back to life like never before.

This is the craziest collection of cartoons since Nealy first put paddle to water and pen to paper. The result is a hilarious slice of the outdoor community as extreme and cutting as Nealy was himself.

Many of the illustrations have not been seen since they were first published. Now they're back and will certainly delight old and new Nealy fans alike. We've taken care to make sure the flow of Nealy's stories and illustrations work just as well in this new format as they did when they were first published years ago.

We are proud at Menasha Ridge Press and AdventureKEEN to help return Nealy's art and irreverent illustrations to the bookshelf. Nealy had a gift for teaching, storytelling, and capturing the beauty of the rivers he sketched and the people he loved. His humorous approach to telling the twisted tales of paddlers, mountain bikers, hikers, campers, inline skaters, and skiers everywhere is a gift to all participating in the weird, wonderful world of outdoor sports.

You can learn more about William, his art, and his many books at thewilliamnealy.com.

SINCERELY,
THE MENASHA RIDGE
PRESS TEAM

## Acknowledgements

Those without whom this book wouldn't have been possible... John Barbour, Lynn Brandon, Wayne-Bob Colwell, Mark Cwick, Dave Schmidt, Nantahala Outdoor Center, Bob Sehlinger, Henry Unger, Barrie Wallace, James Torrence, Tom Schlinkert, and "Bruce".

Very special thanks to my orthopaedist, Dr. Edwin Preston for patching me up every few months, to Gordon Sumerel and the Pedal Power bike shop for keeping my bikes running, and to Dr. Peter Perault for keeping me relatively sane.

Lastly and not leastly, eternal gratitude & love to my main muse, Holly Wallace...

## A Note from the Author...

Dear Dudes and Dudettes,

This is not a book about correct mountain bike riding technique. Fortunately for us, there is no such thing as "correct" mountain biking. Rather, this is a journal of my misadventures on mountain bikes over the last ten years, the reading of which may help you avoid some of my mistakes and perhaps even take a short-cut on the mountain bike learning curve.

Despite my cartoon portrayal of it, mountain biking is not an inherently dangerous sport. However, there are (like me) inherently dangerous mountain bike riders. If you ride out of control you will, like me, probably experience the karmic consequences of out-of-controlness in the form of concussions, separated shoulders, broken collarbones, cracked ribs, sprained wrists, 3rd degree road burns, and lacerations too numerous to mention.

It took me about nine years and a few Kestrels' worth of medical bills to finally ascertain the precepts of safe, sane riding: ① Always wear a helmet! ( I hate them too ), ② Ride in control whenever possible ( sometimes you just gotta hot dog!), ③ Seek to minimize your impact on the natural environment ( repair trail damage, use established trails, don't shred meadows, etc.), ④ Refrain from running into, spooking, and/or alienating pedestrians, hikers, horses, horse people, and wildlife, ⑤ Keep a well-lubed chain, and ⑥ Have as much fun as you can reasonably tolerate!

Kowabunga,

W. Nealy

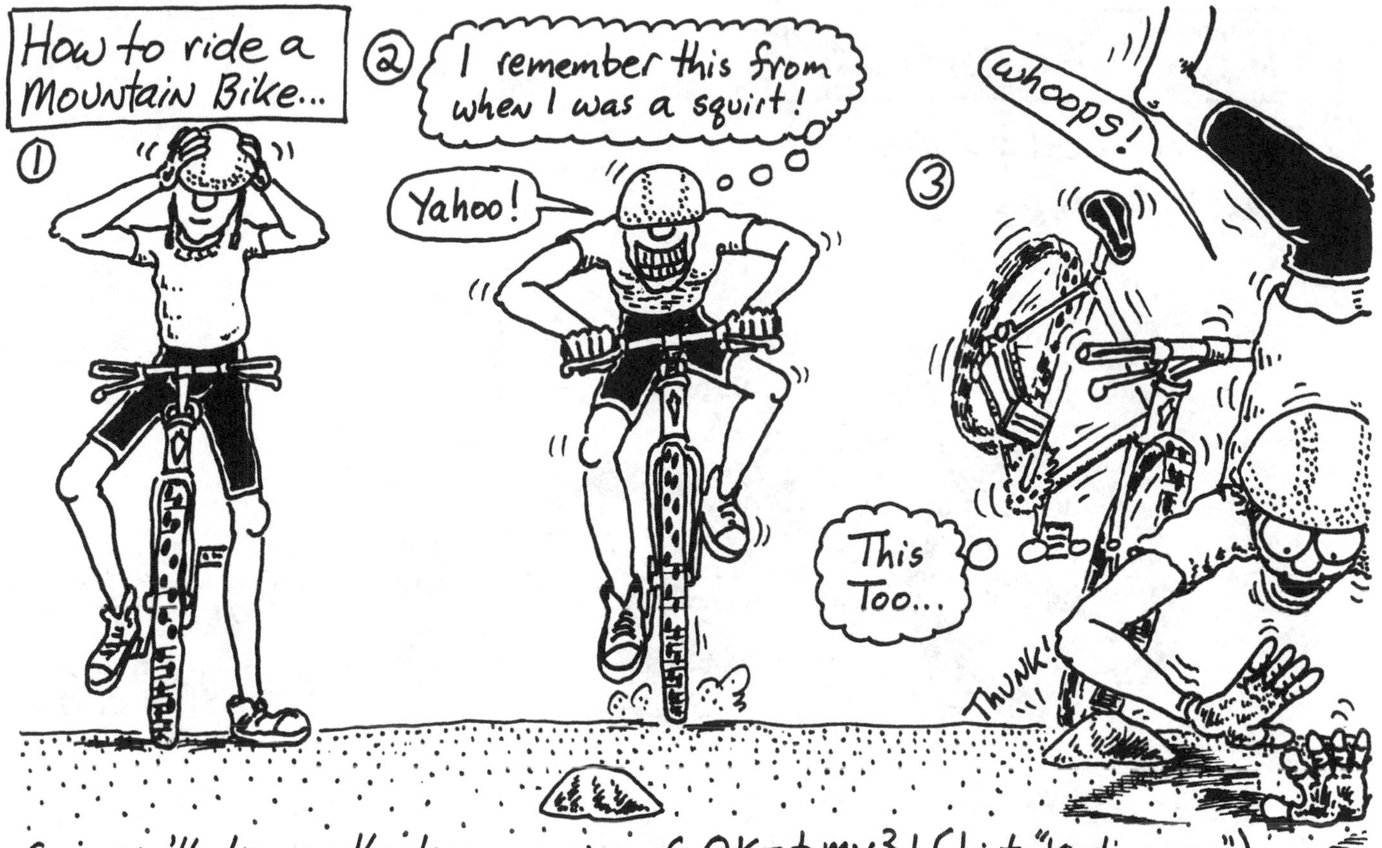
How to ride a Mountain Bike...
1
2
I remember this from when I was a squirt!
Yahoo!
3
whoops!
This Too...
THUNK!

Soon you'll discover the true meaning of $QK = \frac{1}{2}mv^2$! (hint; "kinetic energy")

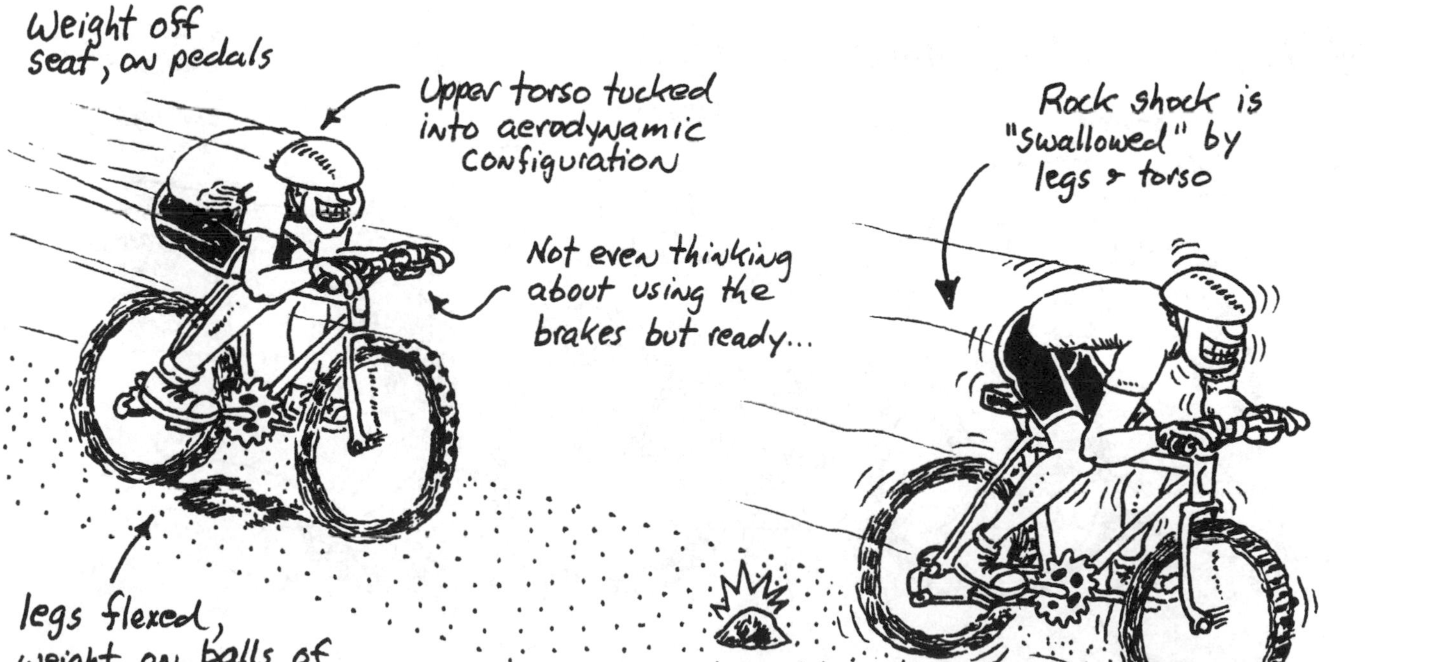
Weight off seat, on pedals
Upper torso tucked into aerodynamic configuration
Not even thinking about using the brakes but ready...
Rock shock is "swallowed" by legs & torso
legs flexed, weight on balls of feet, foot position slightly pigeon-toed
FUP!

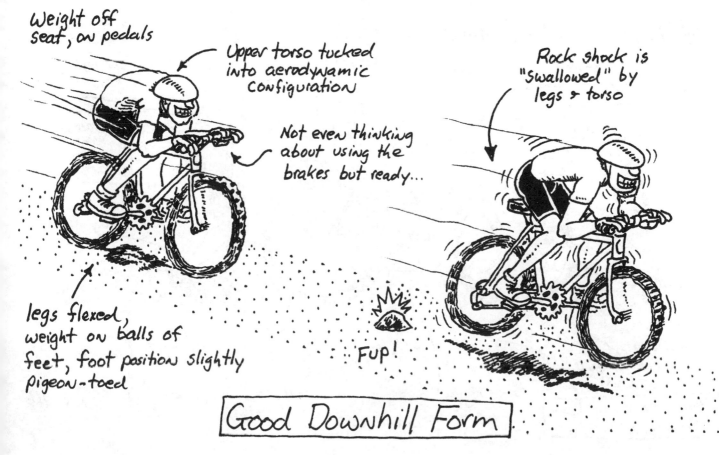

Good Downhill Form

# Mtn. Bike "All The Way"

① Take a good quality mountain bike...

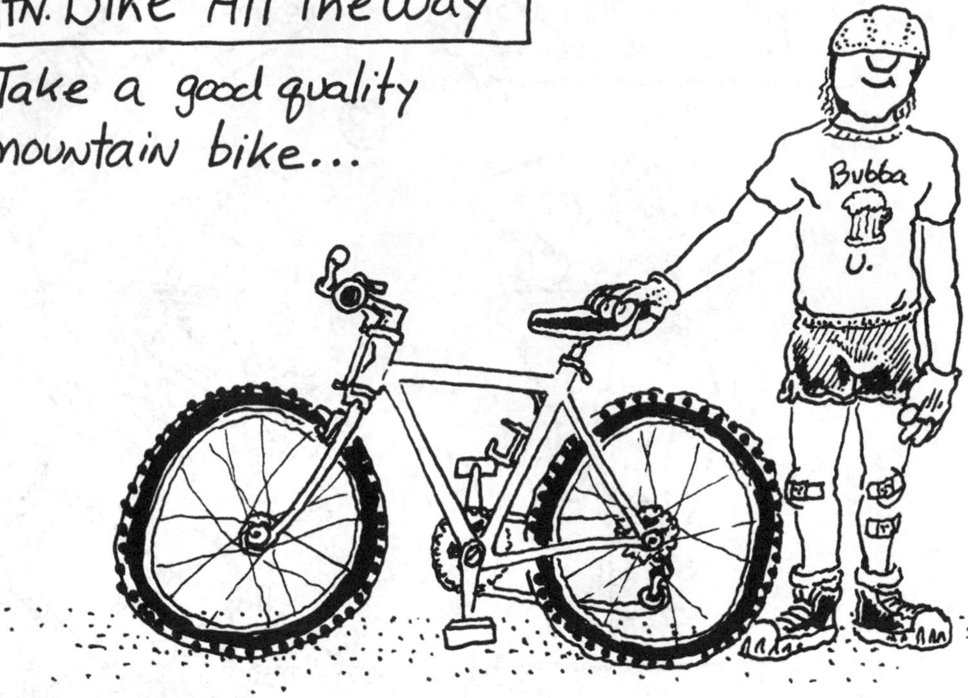
Bubba
U.

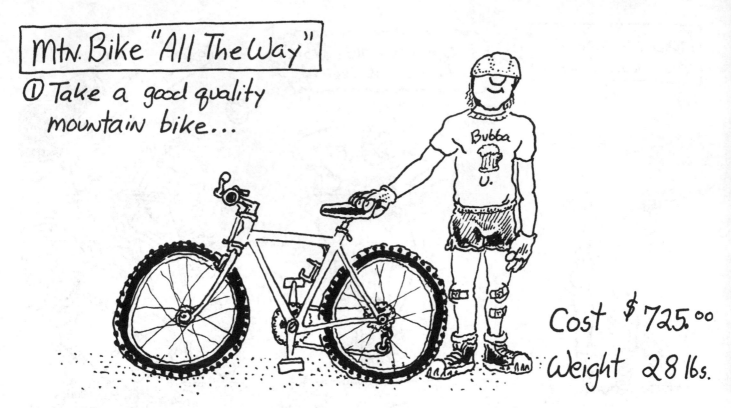

Cost $725.00

Weight 28 lbs.

A defense contractor approach to a more sophisticated all-terrain all-aspect individual-rider two-wheeled personnel carrier.

② Throw a lot of money at it...

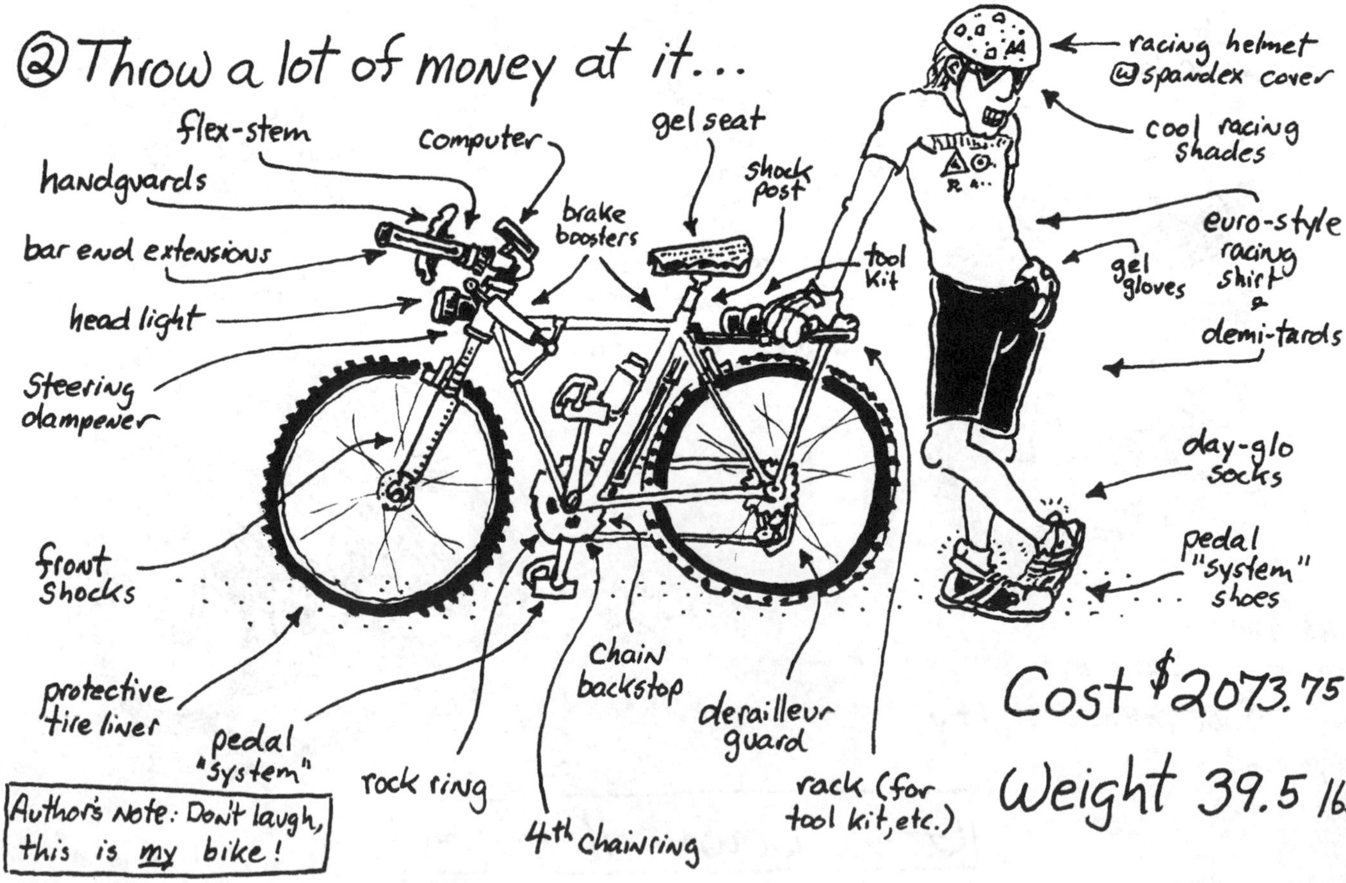
flex-stem
computer
gel seat
handguards
brake boosters
shock post
bar end extensions
tool kit
head light
steering dampener
front shocks
protective tire liner
pedal "system"
rock ring
4th chainring
chain backstop
derailleur guard
rack (for tool kit, etc.)
racing helmet @ spandex cover
cool racing shades
euro-style racing shirt & demi-tards
gel gloves
day-glo socks
pedal "system" shoes

Cost $2073.75

Weight 39.5 lbs.

Author's note: Don't laugh, this is *my* bike!

# Shift Discipline

When riding on steep rolling terrain, staying in low and coasting in the troughs can result in chain suck in the trough as well as a wobble/crash if you try a hard pedal stroke on a low gear at speed. (See "pedalling air", "beartrapped")

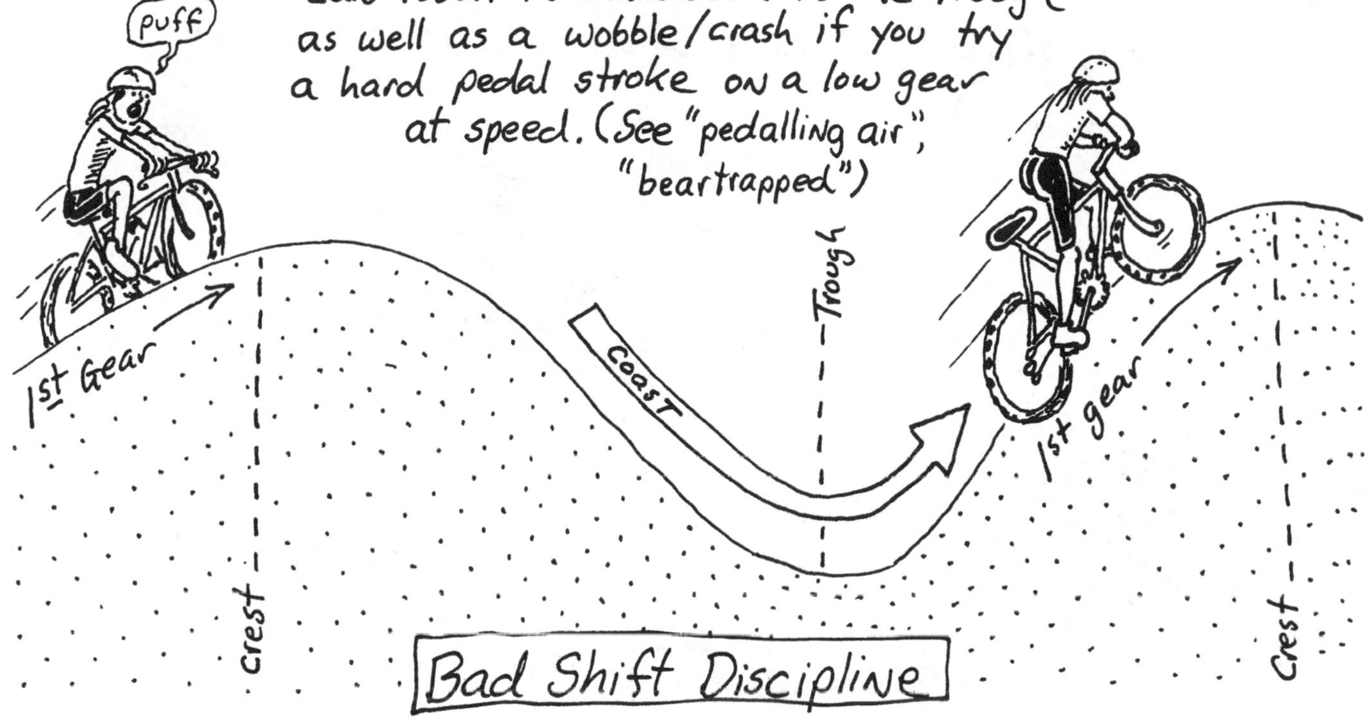

puff
1st Gear
crest
Coast
Trough
1st gear
crest


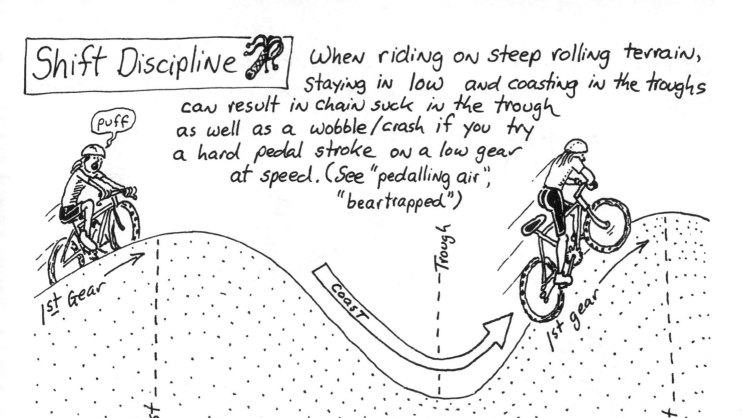

Bad Shift Discipline

To lessen the chances of chain suck in the trough and/or injury to your Naughty parts by pedalling air, use your gears... that's what they are there for. Under almost all conditions, use the highest gear possible.* (See "Pedalling Air")

*Obviously I'm not saying to use every gear on each and every little hill, just the gear appropriate to your velocity on average.

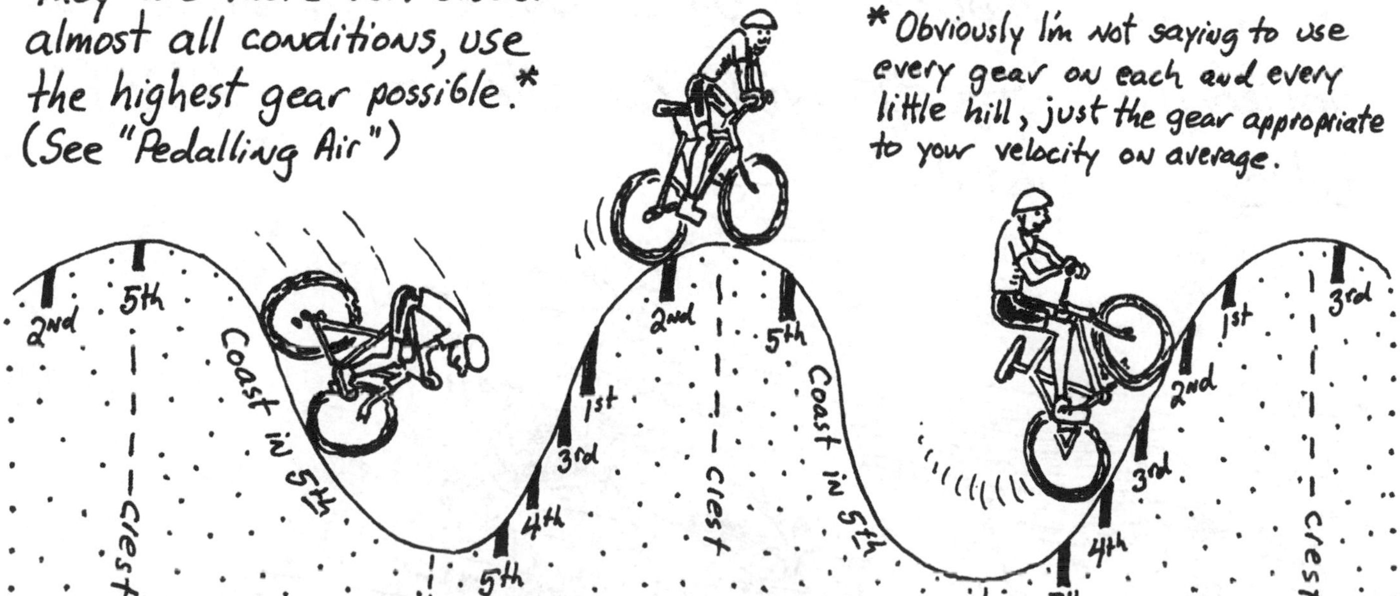

2nd
5th
crest
Coast in 5th
trough
5th
4th
3rd
1st
2nd
5th
crest
Coast in 5th
trough
5th
4th
3rd
2nd
1st
3rd
crest


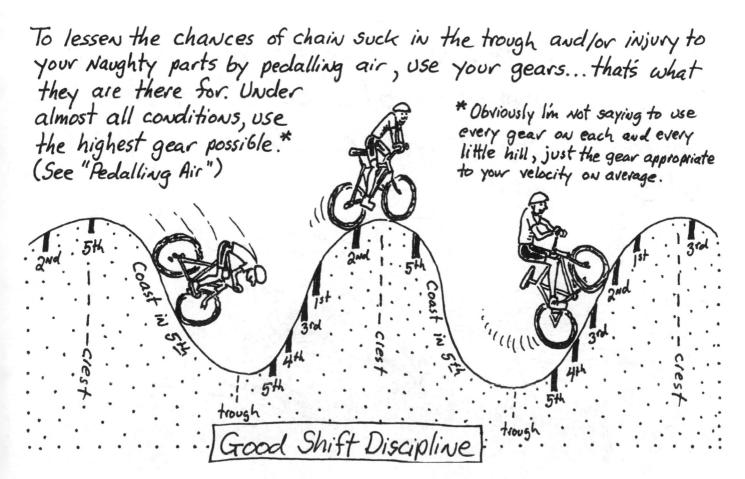

Good Shift Discipline

Scream (skrēm) v. To achieve a velocity such that all rules of common sense and safety are thoroughly violated. Penultimate Fun! (a.k.a. "Bomb")

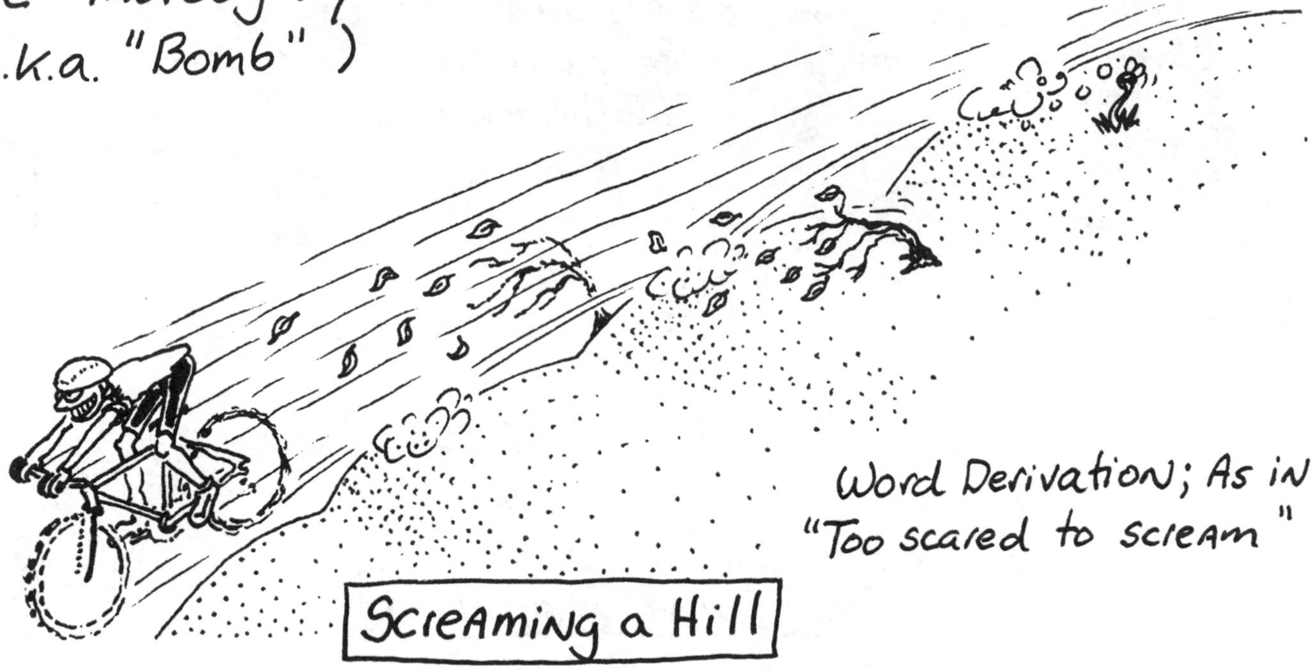

Word Derivation; As in "Too scared to scream"

Screaming a Hill

Poled (pōl•d) v., To be abruptly separated from one's mountain bike by a free-standing horizontal object lying parallel to path of bike. See "First Aid".

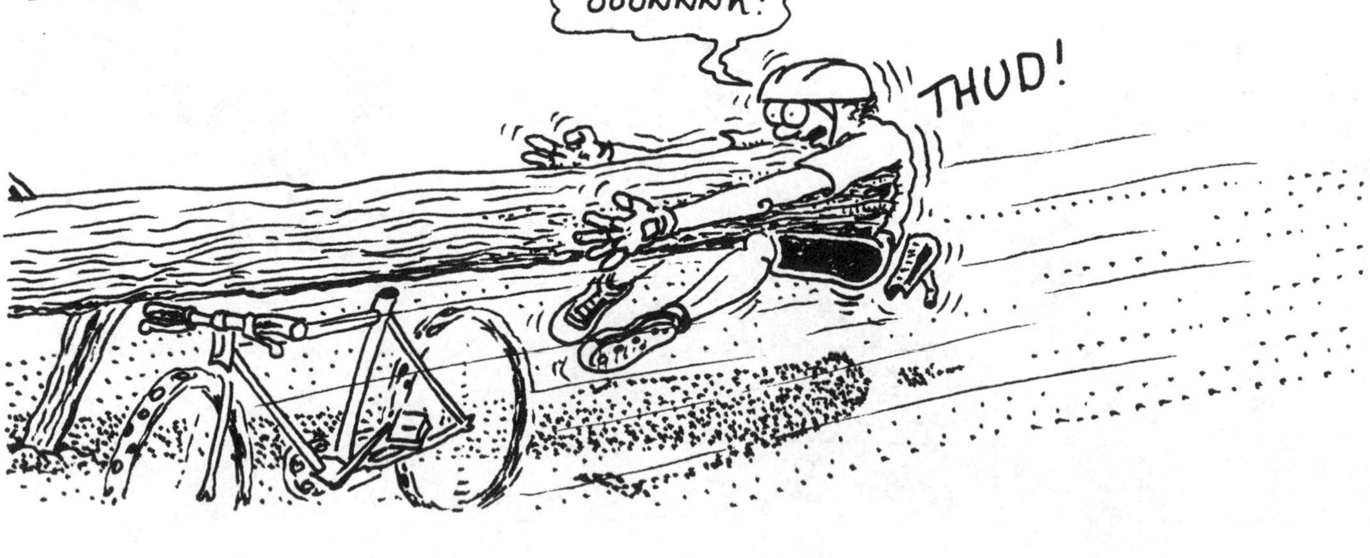

UUUNNNh!
THUD!

## Suspended Log Jumping

Pivot the bike *before* the chain-ring contacts the log, rock bike off log.

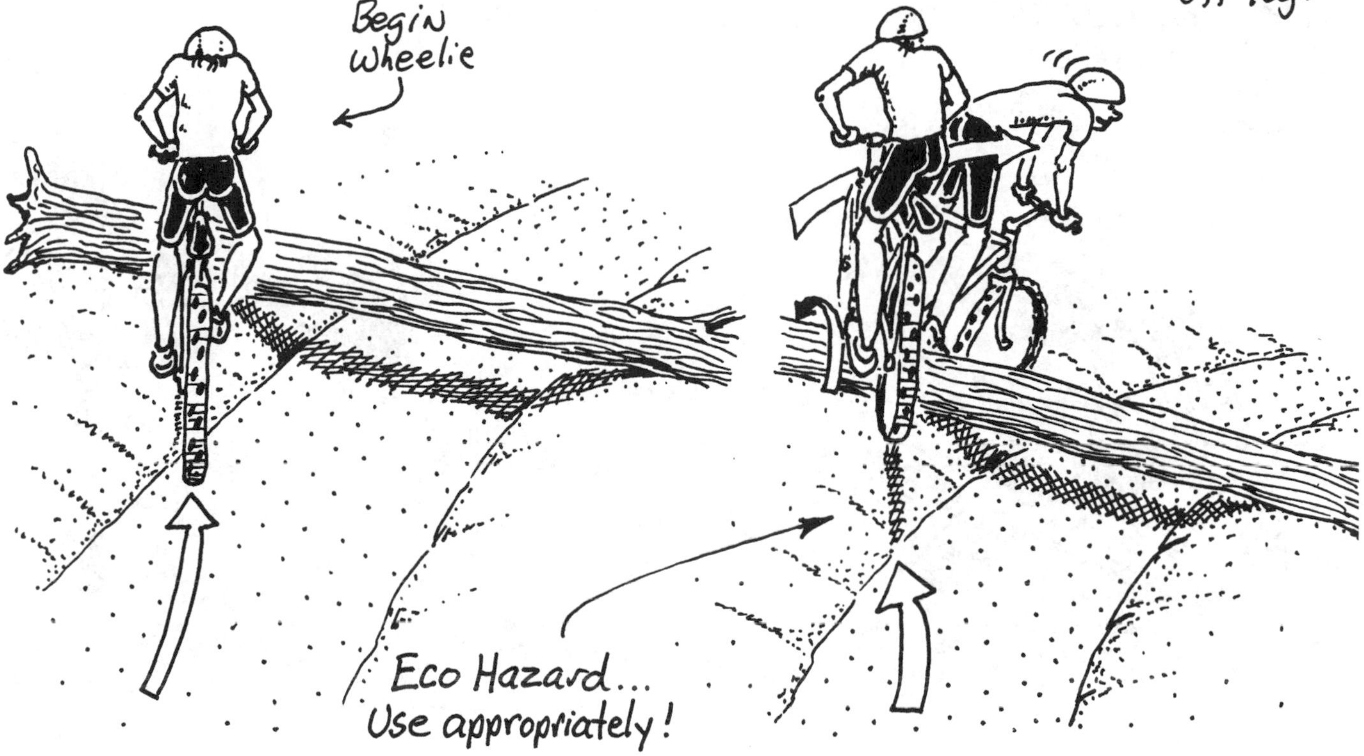
Begin wheelie
Eco Hazard...
Use appropriately!

## Front Wheel Dyno-turn

If you don't want to chance locking your front wheel on steep stuff, lock the rear wheel and *carefully* turn your front wheel sideways. This should bring your bike per-pendicular to the fall line.

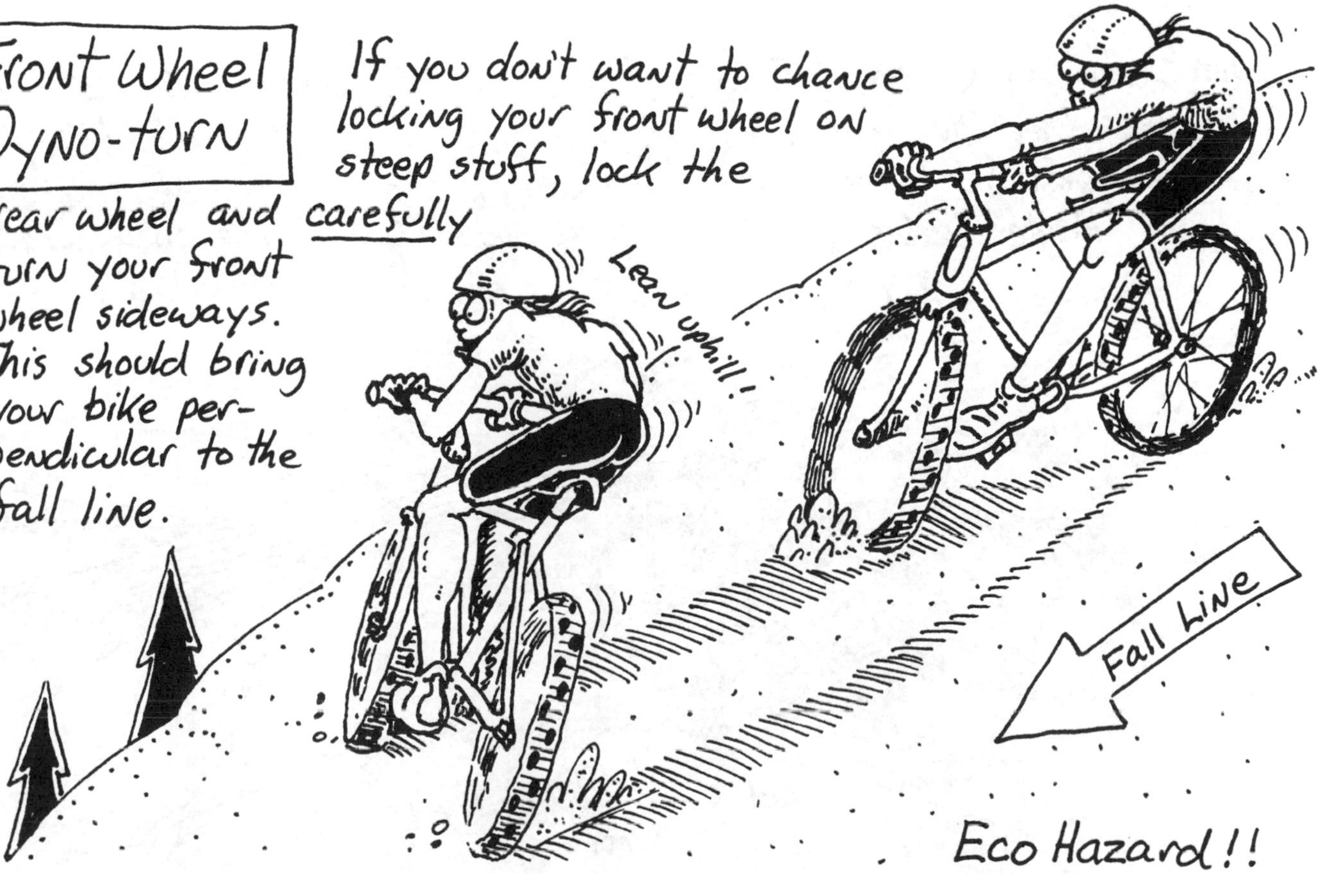
Lean uphill!!
Fall Line
Eco Hazard!!

Dab (dăb) v., To touch any portion of one's anatomy to the ground while riding in a trials-like manner. See "face plant" etc.

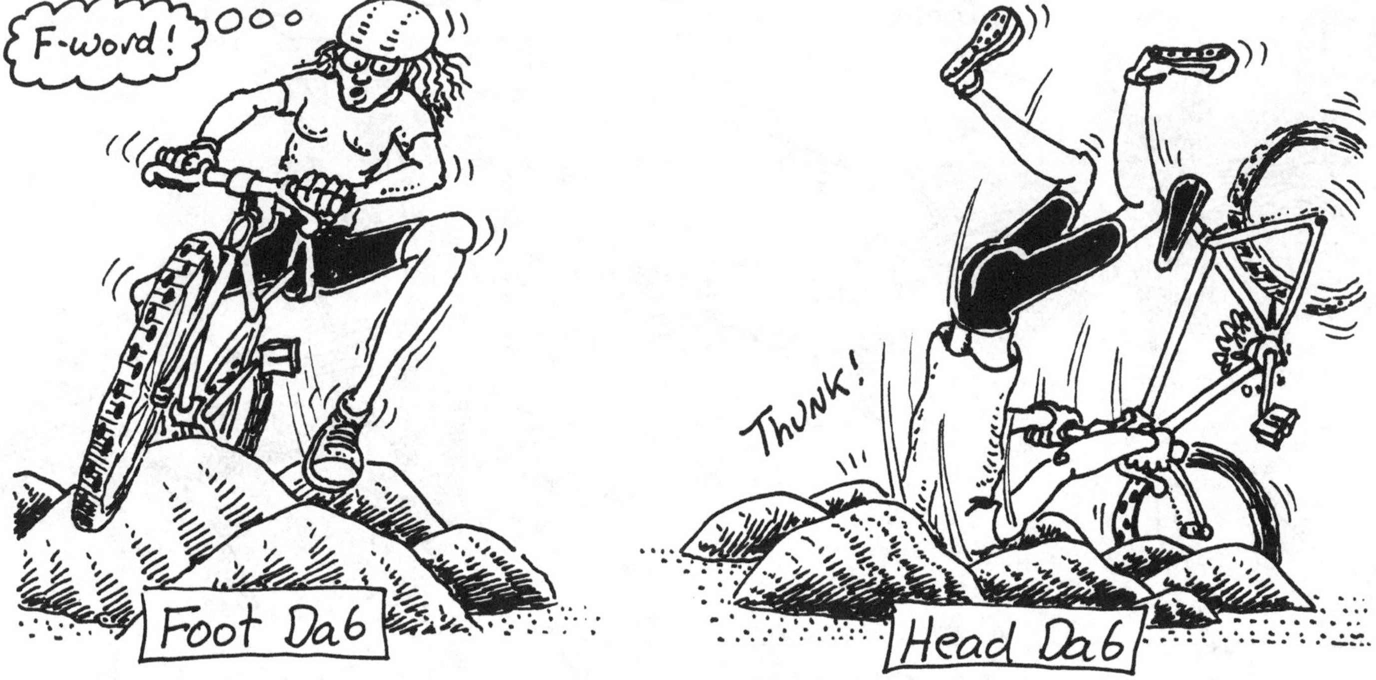
F-word!
Foot Dab
THUNK!
Head Dab

Limbo Log (lêm·bō lôg) n., (a.k.a. "deadfall", etc.) A log or other organic obstacle crossing a trail horizontally with several feet of space between log & ground. Misjudge one of these babies, even at slow speeds, and it's ouch-o-rama! See "clotheslined"

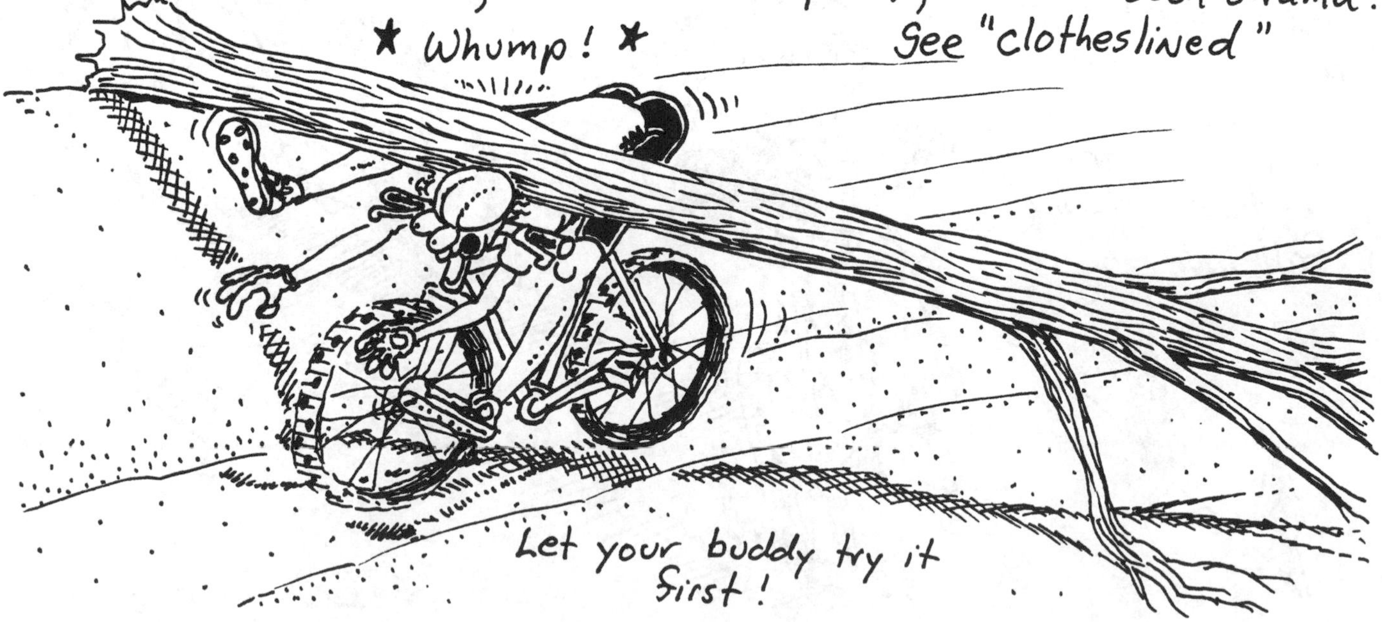
* Whump! *
Let your buddy try it first!

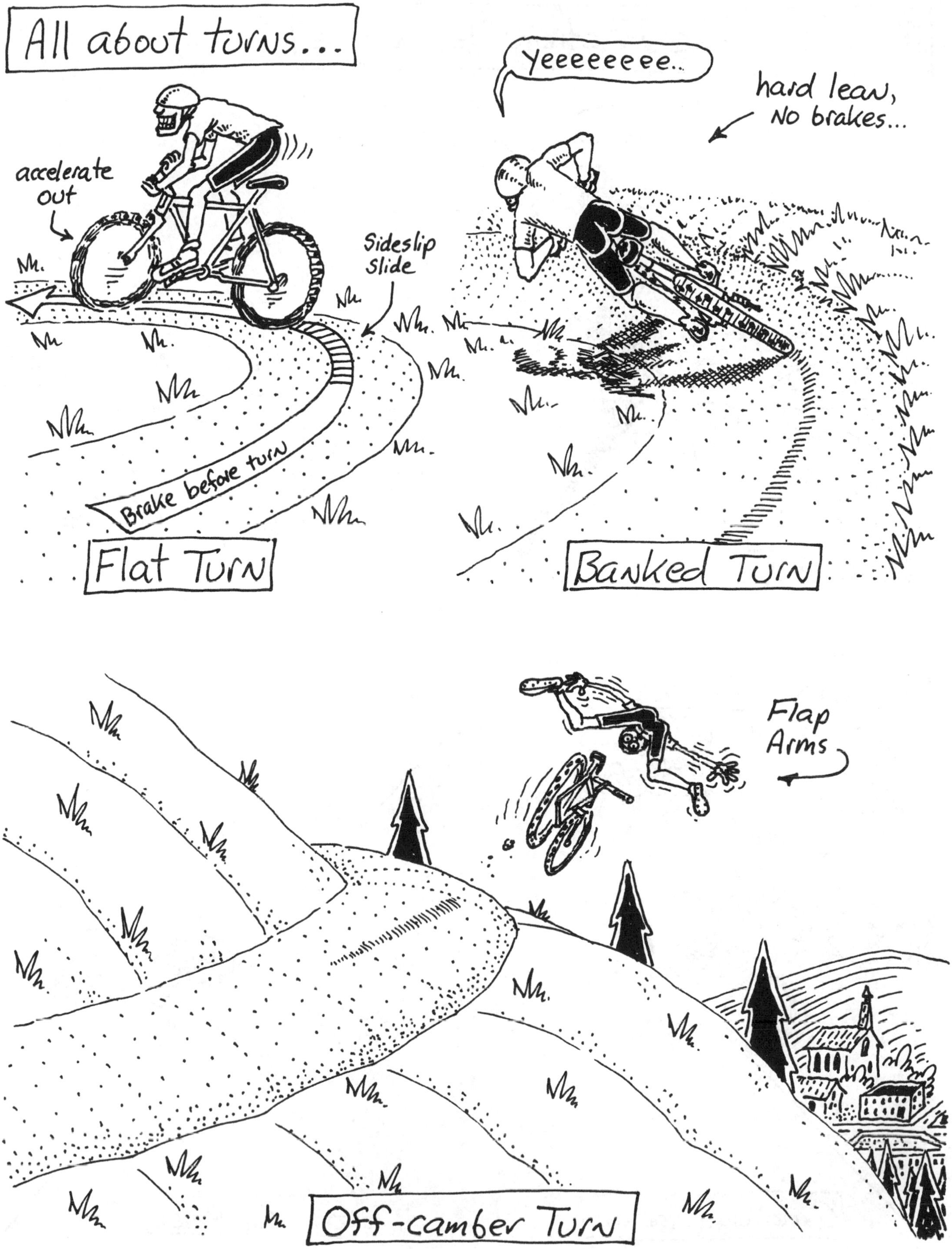
All about turns...
accelerate out
Sideslip slide
Brake before turn
Flat Turn
yeeeeeeee..
hard lean, No brakes...
Banked Turn
Flap Arms
Off-camber Turn

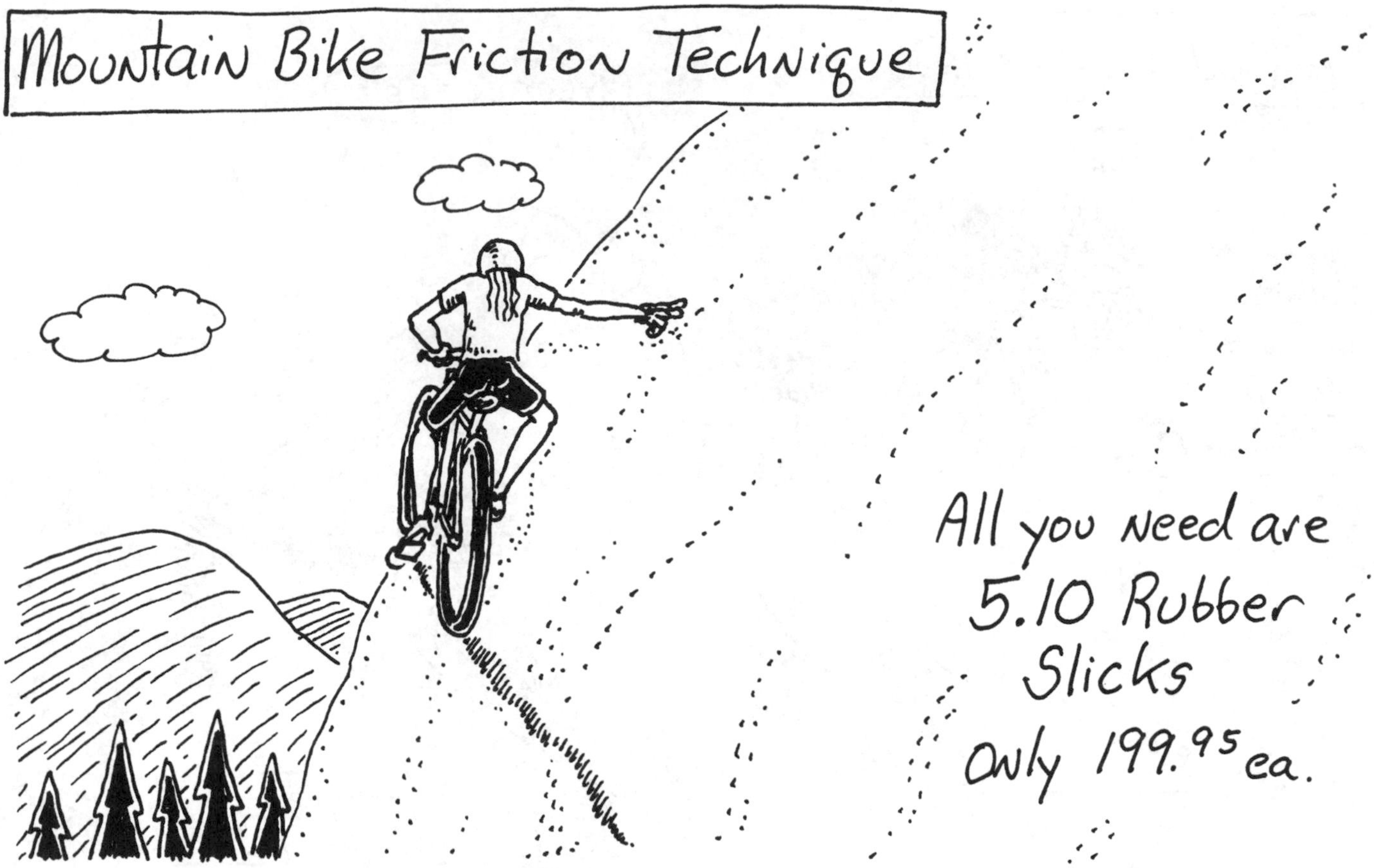
Mountain Bike Friction Technique
All you need are 5.10 Rubber Slicks Only 199.95 ea.

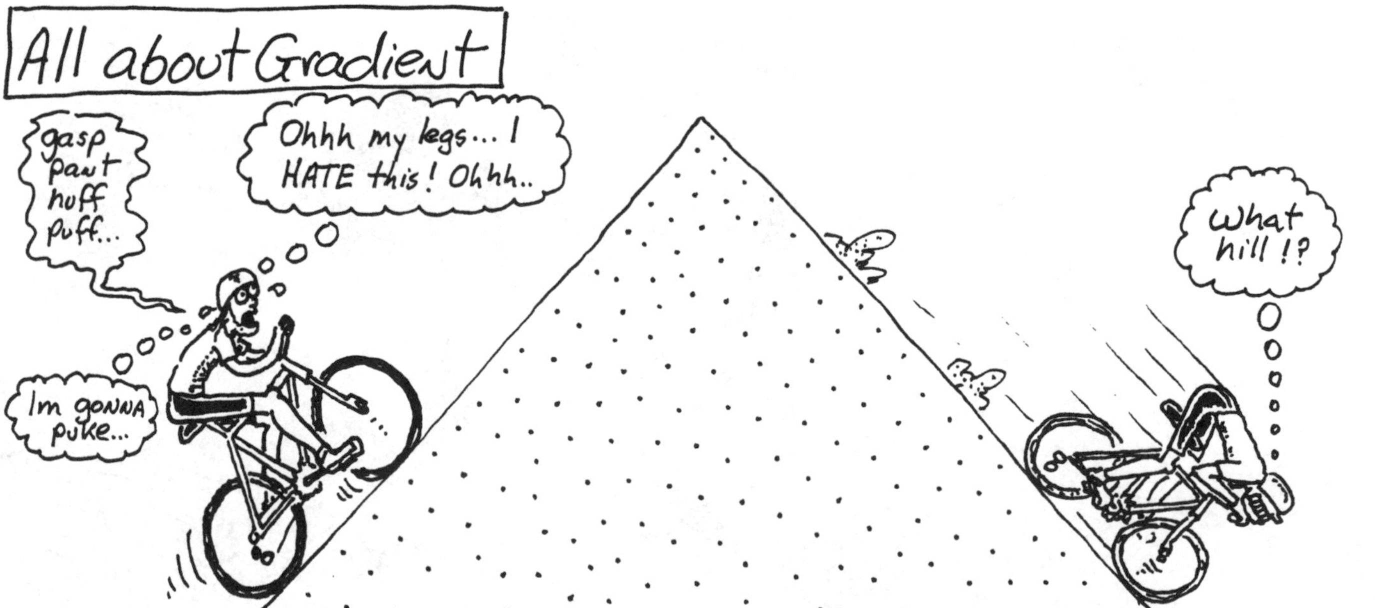
All about Gradient
gasp pant huff puff...
Ohhh my legs... I HATE this! Ohhh..
Im gonna puke...
What hill!?
Gradient Storage
Gradient Release

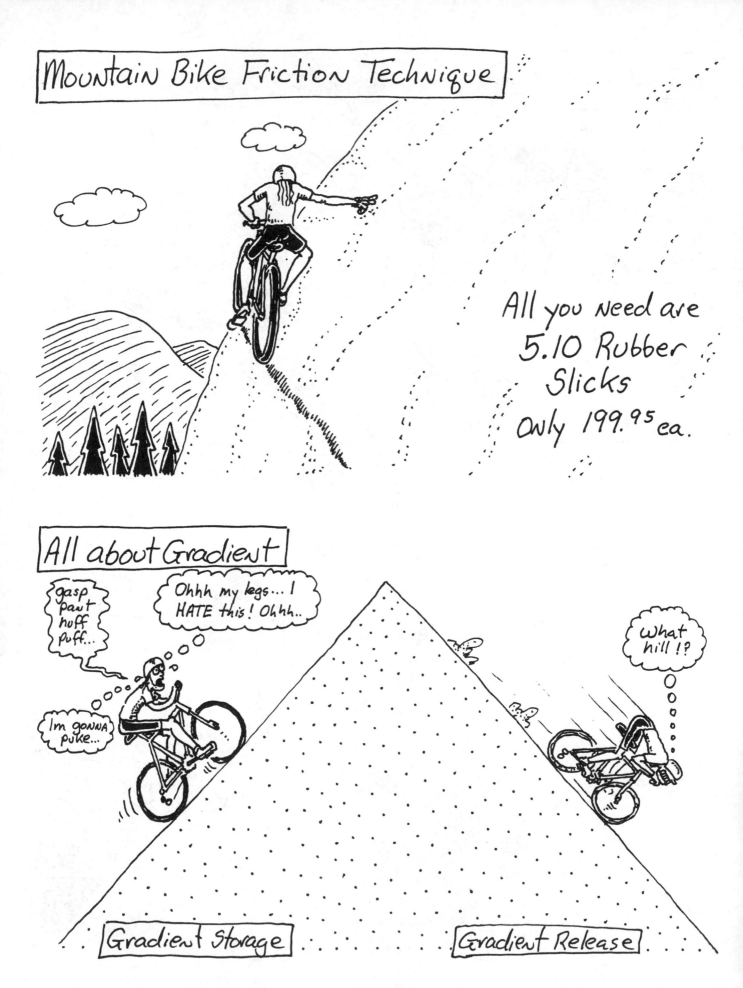

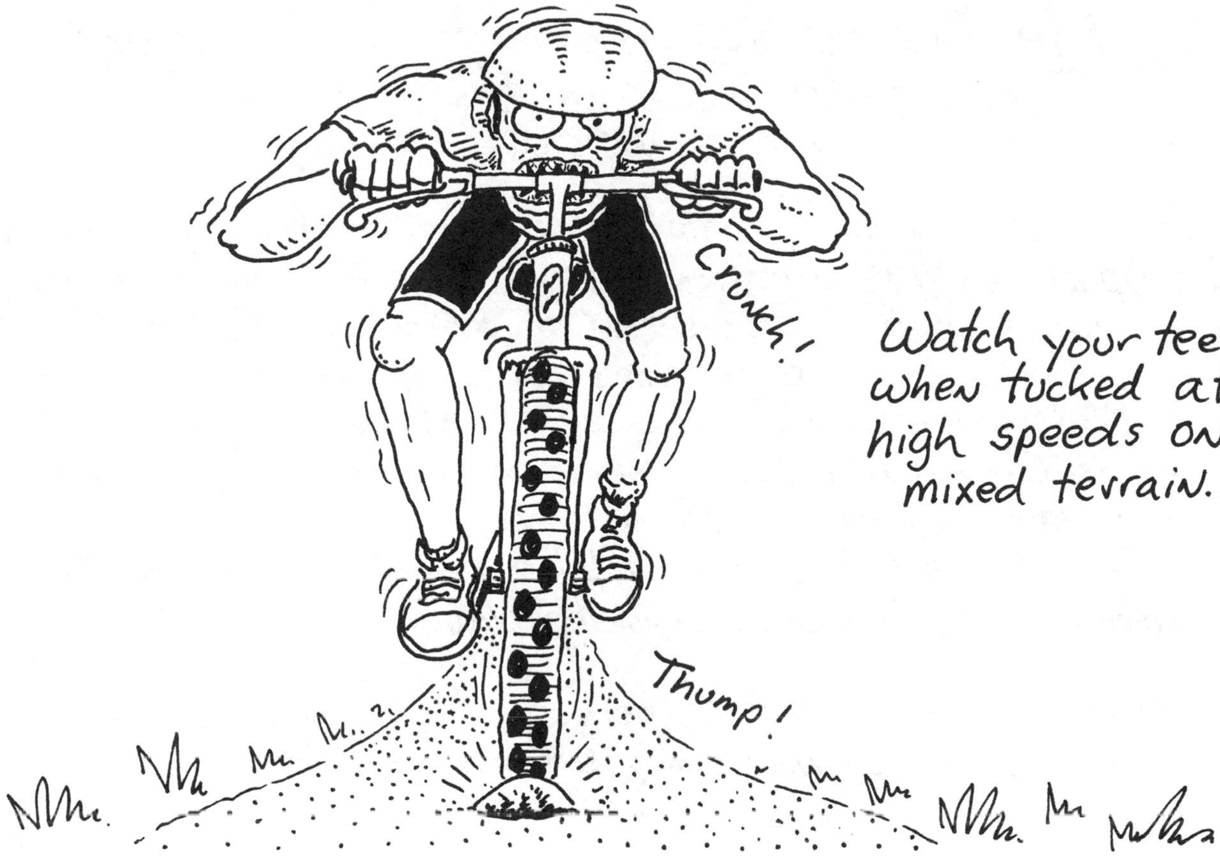
Crunch!
Thump!

Watch your teeth when tucked at high speeds on mixed terrain...

Hammered (hâm·merde) (a.k.a. "crash & burn")
Any particularly picturesque total body wipeout with aerial maneuvers. (see "face plant" "body carve", etc. also "first aid")

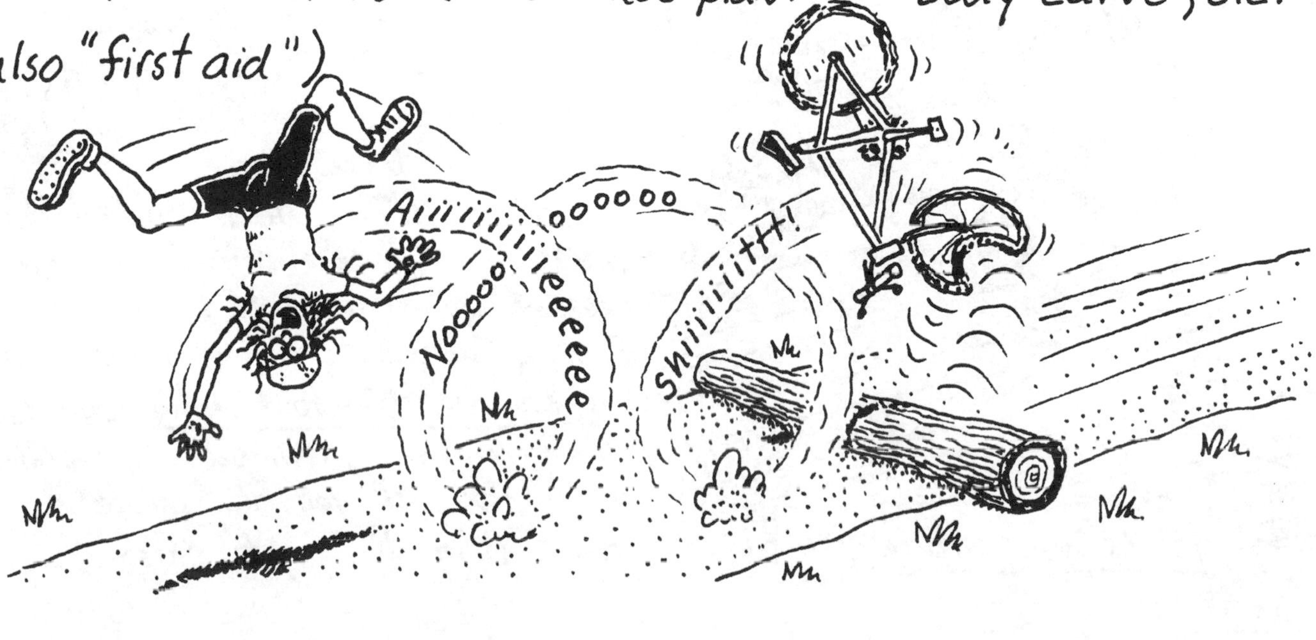
Aiiiiiiiiiieeeeee
Noooooo
oooooo
Shiiiiiitt!

# The First Winter Descent of the Third or Fourth Highest Peak in the Great Smoky Mountains National Park

After the <u>Outside</u> article on mountain biking appeared in the Spring of '79, my friend Bruce*and I acquired a couple old Schwinns and proceeded to demolish both the bikes and ourselves. Our favorite activities were high-speed pedestrian slalo and staircase-riding on the campus of the University of North Ca olina in Chapel Hill. And drinking beer. In short, we were bad boys in need of serious punishment.

That December Bruce, Holly' and I drove to Alabama for Christmas via the Great Smokies National Park. Bruce and I

*I can't use Bruce's last name because he's an electrical engineer wit a defense contractor now and probably wants to remain so.
' See bottom of next page

Hi ladies!

Whoops

What an idiot!

UNC Campus, circa 1979

had been planning a little side excursion. On the eastern end of the park there's a foot trail running off Mt. Sterling (5,842') to Big Creek Campground with an average gradient of 1,000 feet per mile for six odd miles. A couple years earlier I had hiked it. Baxter Creek Trail was a grunt, pure and simple, going up. Bruce and I planned to bomb down it.

At 3:30 PM we unloaded the bikes on a saddle a forest service road crossed within a couple miles of the Mt. Sterling Firetower, visible 1,000' above the saddle. We told Holly we'd see

' My permanent girlfriend. ("Woman-friend" for all you P.C.* dweebs...
* P.C. = "Politically Correct" person

her in an hour or so at the campground in the valley below. Bruce and I figured we'd surely beat the car down. After about 200 yds. the jeep trail to the firetower got too steep to pedal a 1-speed cruiser... we began a push/carry bike ascent epic. At about sundown we staggered into the clearing below the firetower. There was snow on the ground and, because Bruce and I had wisely elected to wear only T-shirts and blue jeans (now sweat-soaked) we were getting very cold. Now all we had to do was to select the correct trailhead to the campground from a number of trailheads leading out of the

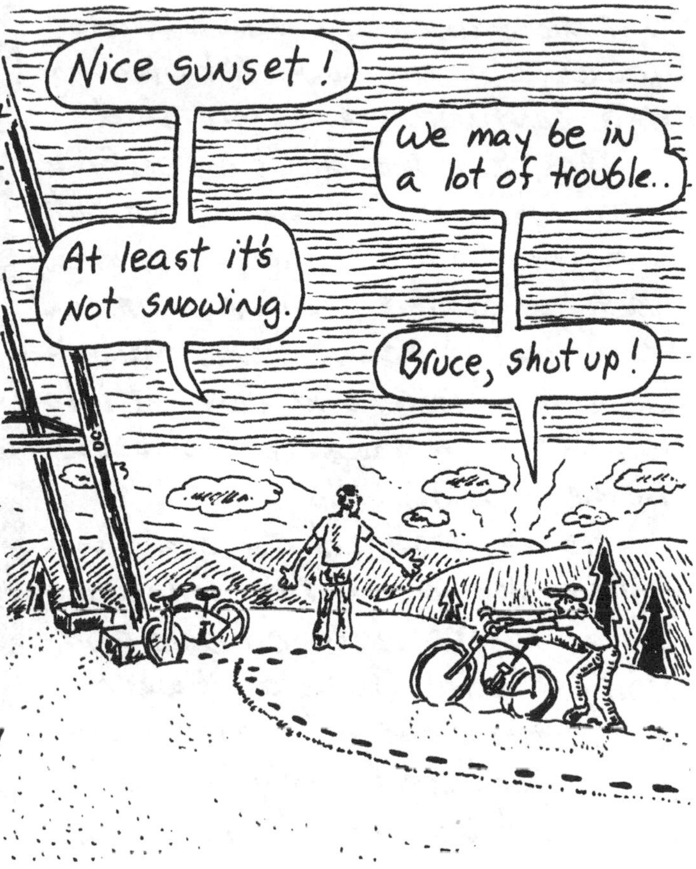

Nice sunset!
We may be in a lot of trouble..
At least it's not snowing.
Bruce, shut up!


clearing, all unmarked. Being hippie radicals, we chose the trailhead farthest left. In fading daylight we said a prayer to the bike gods and took off down the mountain. Bruce led because I couldn't see too well in the gloom in my ultra-dark prescription sunglasses. About ten minutes later I slid around a corner and ran over Bruce's arm, which was lying across the trail where Bruce lay sprawled after having been clotheslined by a fallen spruce tree hanging across the trail. After we finally located Bruce's glasses, which had been knocked off his head in the crash, we resumed the descent.

The trail was so steep we had

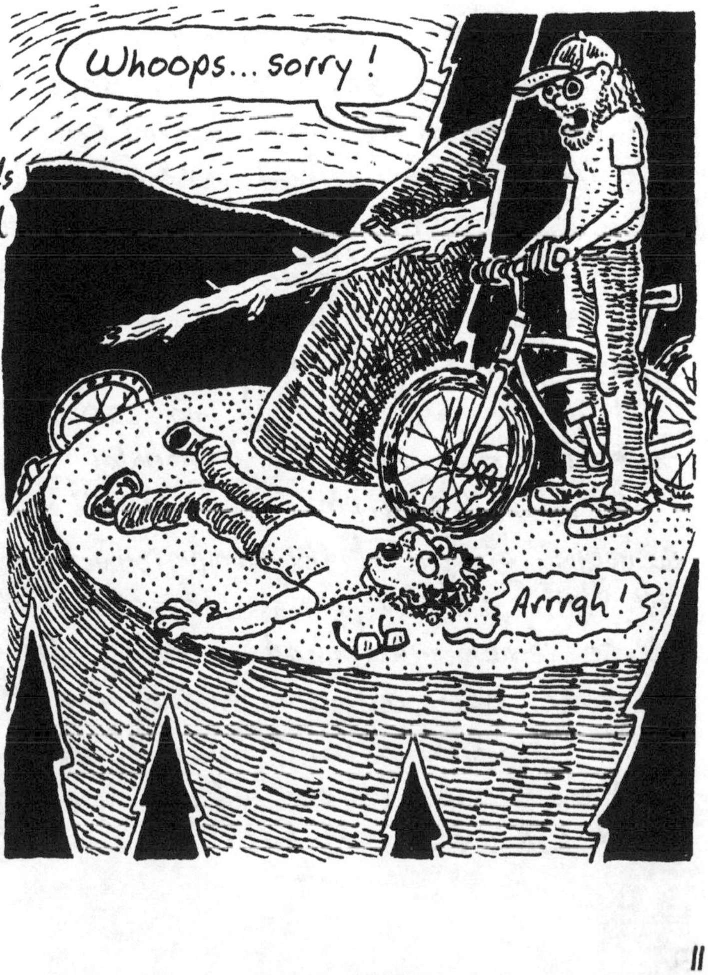

Whoops... sorry!
Arrrgh!

to ride standing on our coaster brakes, coming down Mt. Sterling in a continuous dynamic skid.

"Mayday! Mayday! I'm on FIRE!" Dense white smoke was pouring out of my rear hub. Neither of us knew exactly what this phenomenon meant. I assumed it meant I was fixing to loose my brake and plummet into Big Creek, a thousand feet below in the shadows. Ulp.

As we resumed our semi-controlled skid down Mt. Sterling we began to speculate on ours and Holly's fate. Being as it was dark, below freezing and we were way overdue, Bruce speculated, Holly has probably begun to think seriously about finding

Mayday! Mayday! I'm on FIRE!

a ranger and organizing a rescue party. If she hasn't been raped and murdered by the local mutants, I countered. If we had chosen the correct trail at the top (and therefore weren't hopelessly lost and hypothermic) then, technically, we were merely late and hypothermic. Surely the rangers would only fine us and not cart us directly to a mental institution...

At around 6:30 PM we crossed the swinging bridge at the campground. No Holly, no car, no rangers. Shit! Bruce remembered that, it being late December and all, this end of the park was closed until April. It was two more miles to the entrance gate and we went real fast.

Rescue Squad

Well, miss, I'm gonna transport these here prisoners to the Primate Institute in Atlanta...

Chatter chatter

A vision of Beauty awaited us at the gate: Holly, warm car, cold beer and no rangers in sight. "You are late late late!" Holly said after opening her window about two inches. She took a sip of a steaming cup of coffee and scotch. "I thought you guys were hurt or lost or dead." "Please unlock the doors... pleeeaaassse!" I whimpered "Bruce and I are both very sorry and awfully cold to boot. And we will never even <u>think</u> about doing anything like this ever again!" "Amen" said Bruce.

She started the car. "See you two in Birmingham". She put the car in drive. "It is 350 @★ϟ! miles to Birmingham" I choked, hanging

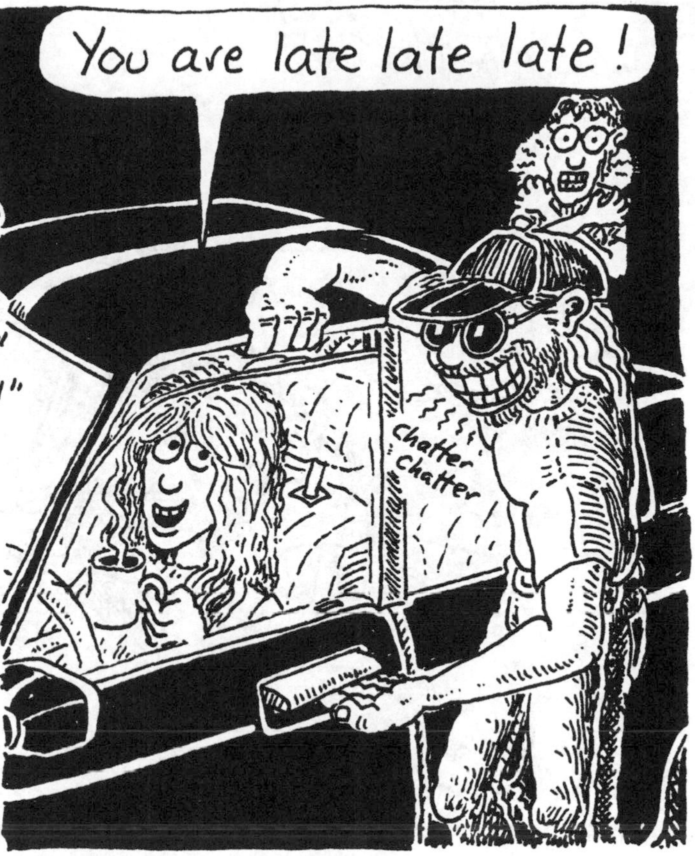

You are late late late!
Chatter Chatter


onto the car with chattering teeth. "Hmm... 350 miles..." she said "Well guys, enjoy!"

Epilogue- She eventually allowed two penitant, frozen mountain bikers into the car after a little more well-deserved humiliation. Bruce has a real job now but rides when he can. I've become a helmeted, lycra-clad safety weenie and, between crashes and injuries, ride in a responsible and dignified manner. For me...

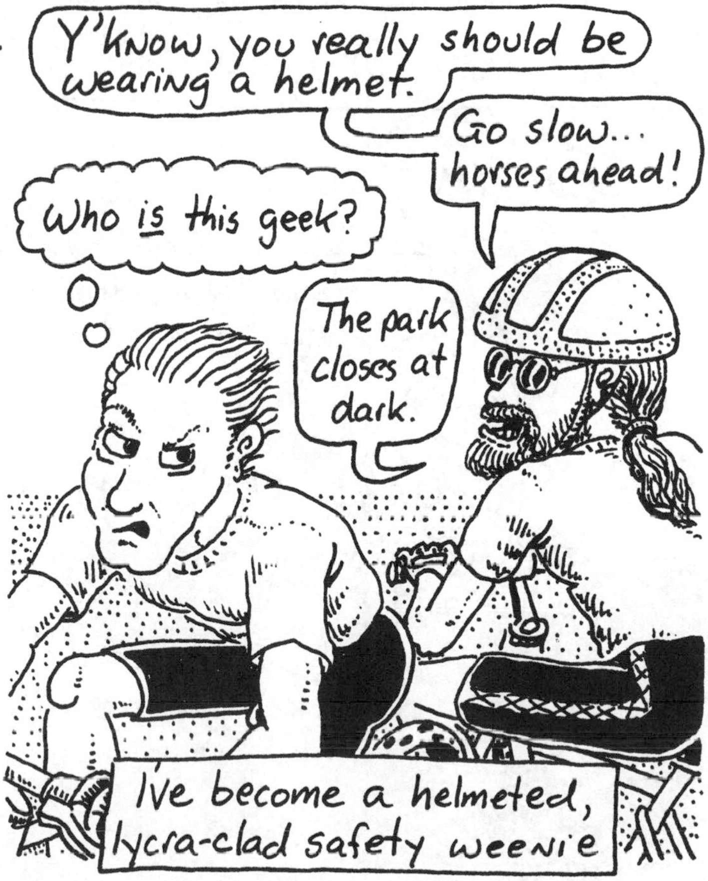

Y'know, you really should be wearing a helmet.
Go slow... horses ahead!
Who is this geek?
The park closes at dark.
I've become a helmeted, lycra-clad safety weenie


The End

P.S. Holly, to this day, refuses to run shuttle!

# Bike Anatomy

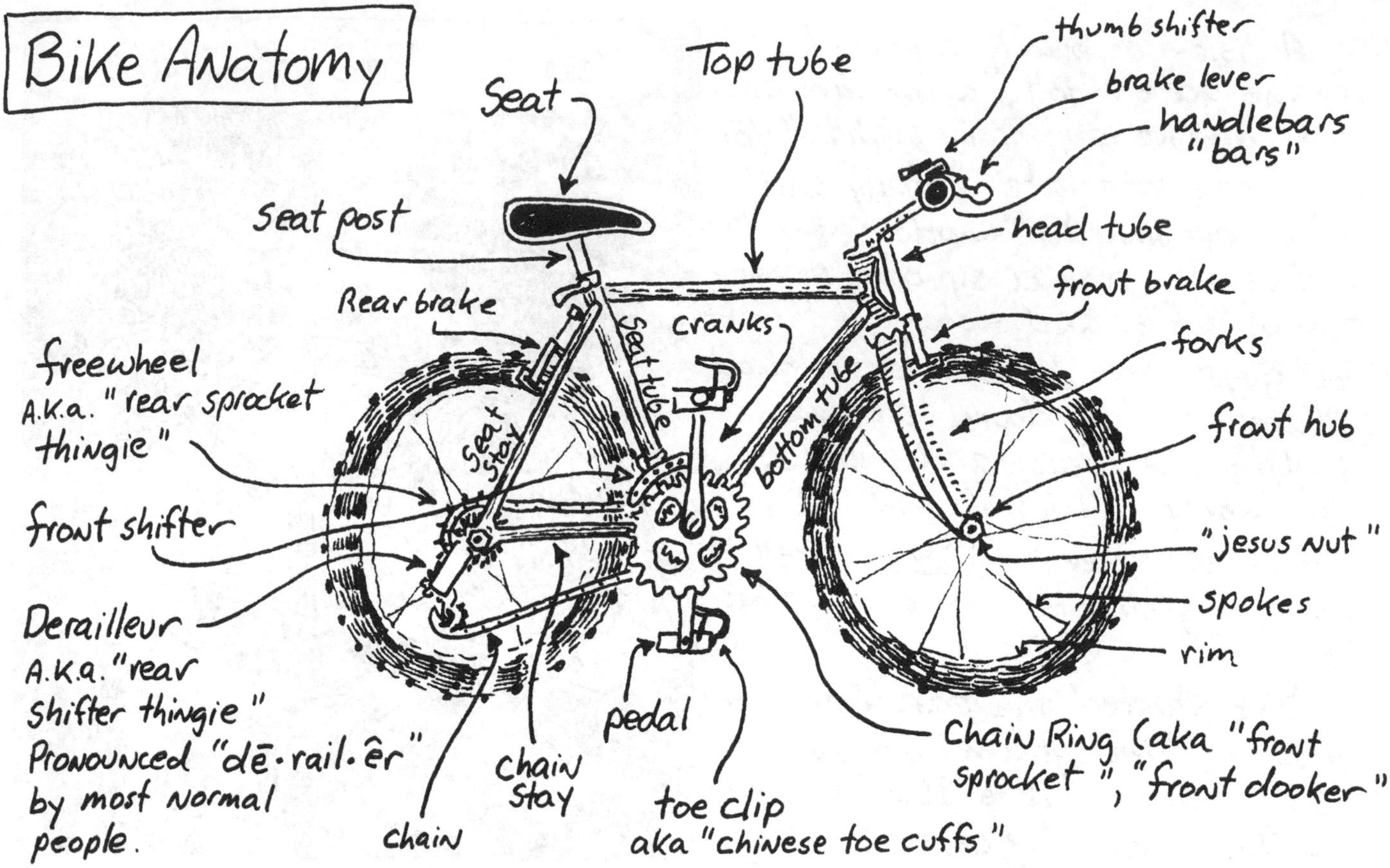
thumb shifter
brake lever
handlebars "bars"
Top tube
Seat
Seat post
head tube
front brake
Rear brake
cranks
forks
freewheel A.k.a. "rear sprocket thingie"
seat tube
seat stay
bottom tube
front hub
front shifter
"jesus nut"
spokes
rim
Derailleur A.k.a. "rear shifter thingie" Pronounced "dē·rail·êr" by most normal people.
pedal
chain stay
chain
toe clip aka "chinese toe cuffs"
Chain Ring (aka "front sprocket", "front dooker"

# Bike anatomy, cont'd..

## Chainring Detail

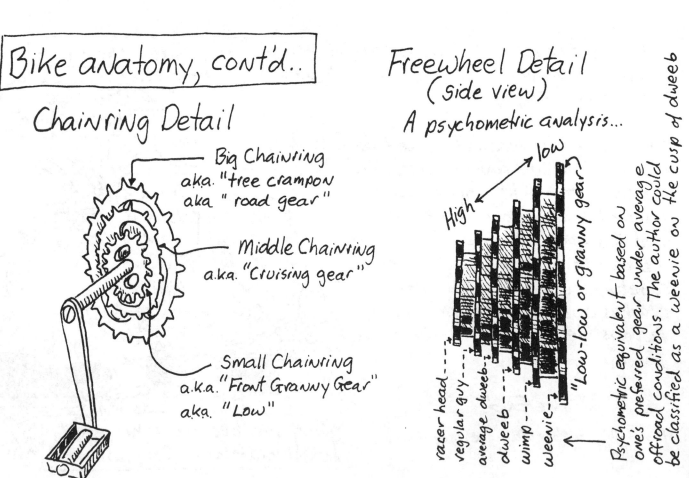

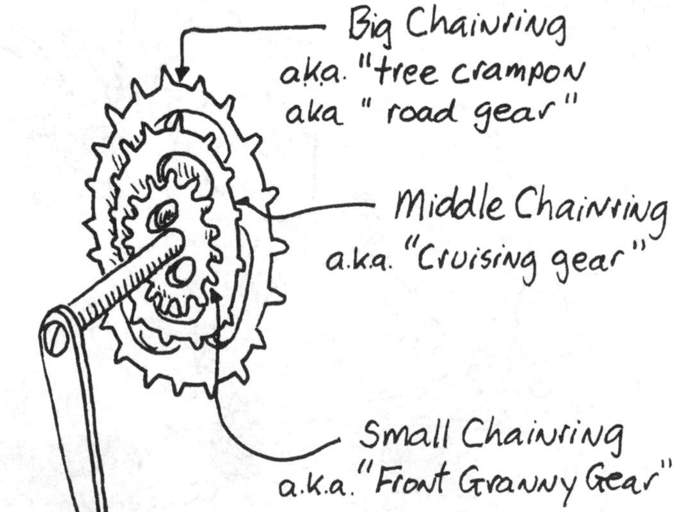
Big Chainring aka. "tree crampon aka " road gear"
Middle Chainring a.k.a. "Cruising gear"
Small Chainring a.k.a. "Front Granny Gear" aka. "Low"

## Freewheel Detail (side view)

A psychometric analysis...

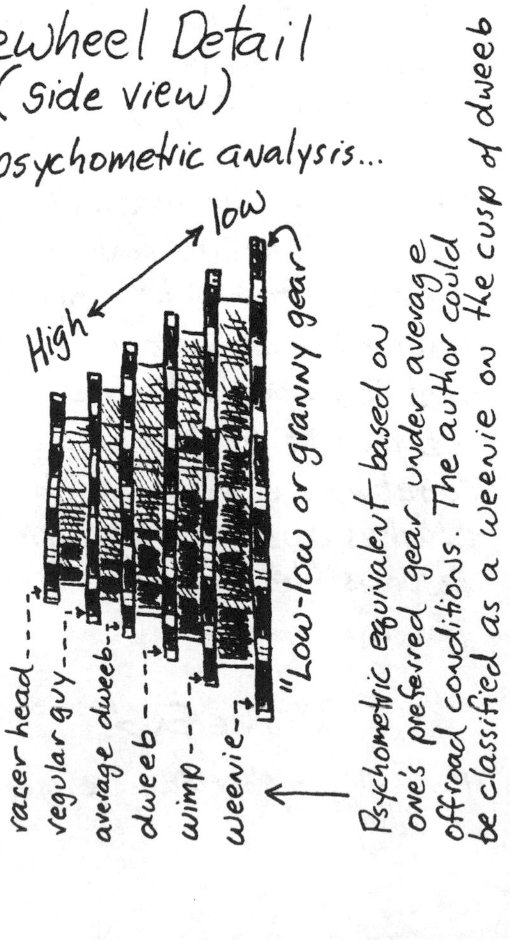
low
High
"Low-low or granny gear"
racer head
regular guy
average dweeb
dweeb
wimp
weenie
Psychometric equivalent based on one's preferred gear under average offroad conditions. The author could be classified as a weenie on the cusp of dweeb

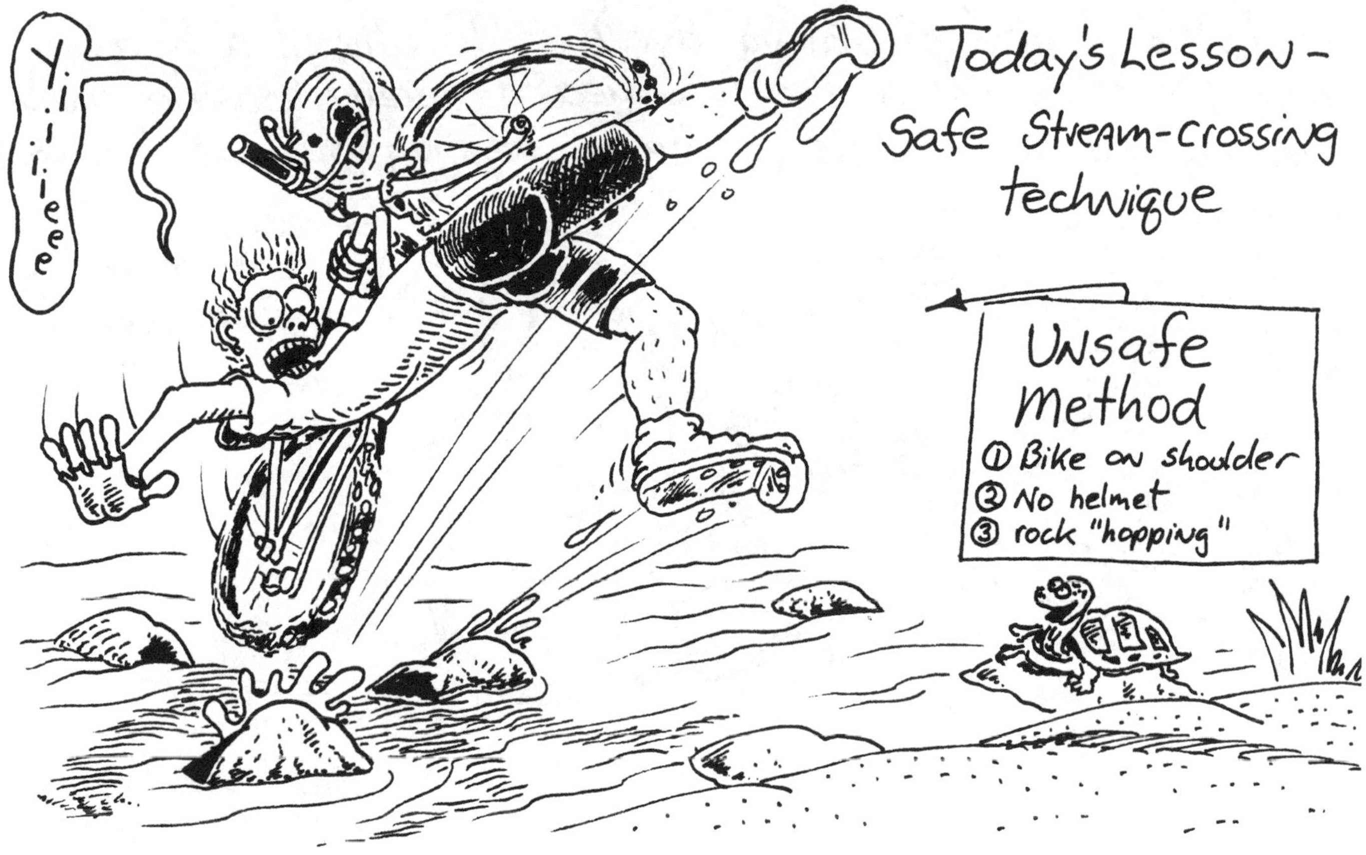
Y-i-i-i-i-eee
Today's Lesson - Safe Stream-crossing technique
Unsafe Method
① Bike on shoulder
② No helmet
③ rock "hopping"

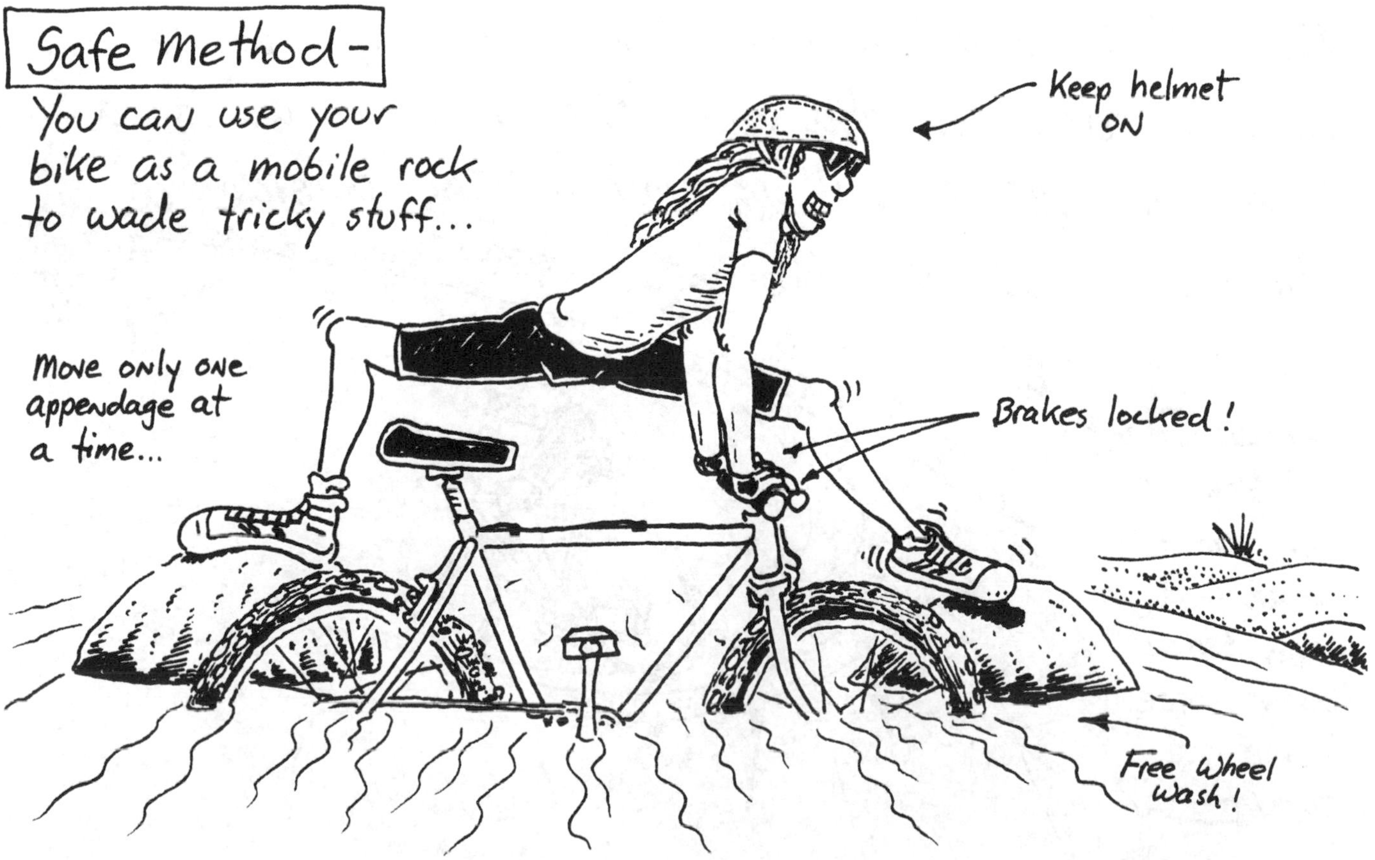
Safe method -
You can use your bike as a mobile rock to wade tricky stuff...
Keep helmet ON
Move only one appendage at a time...
Brakes locked!
Free Wheel wash!

Pedalling Air (pêd·âl·ng âyr) v., To attempt a hard pedal stroke on a too-low gear thereby loosing one's footing on the pedals, perhaps causing sufficient wobble to crash the bike...

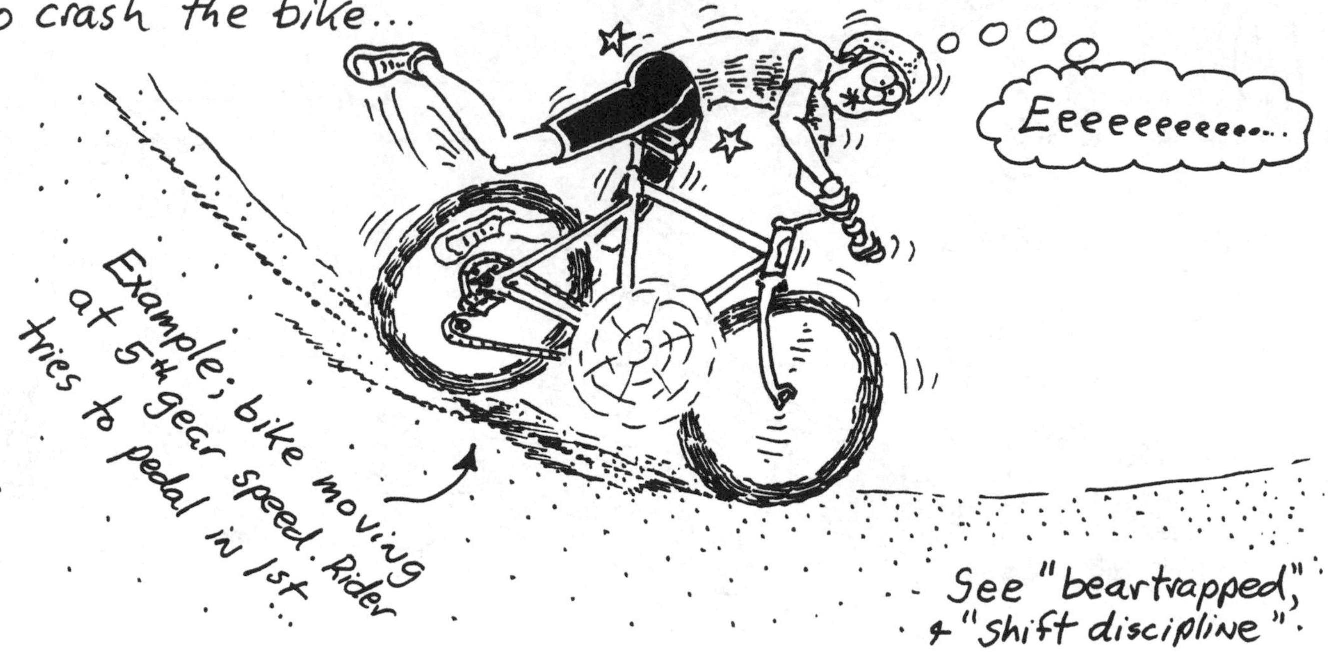

Eeeeeeeeee....
Example; bike moving at 5th gear speed. Rider tries to pedal in 1st...
See "beartrapped", & "shift discipline".


Magnetic Turn (mâg·nê·tîk tûrn) n., A decreasing-radius turn. Inertia will make it seem as if a giant magnet is pulling you to the outside of the turn and over the edge.

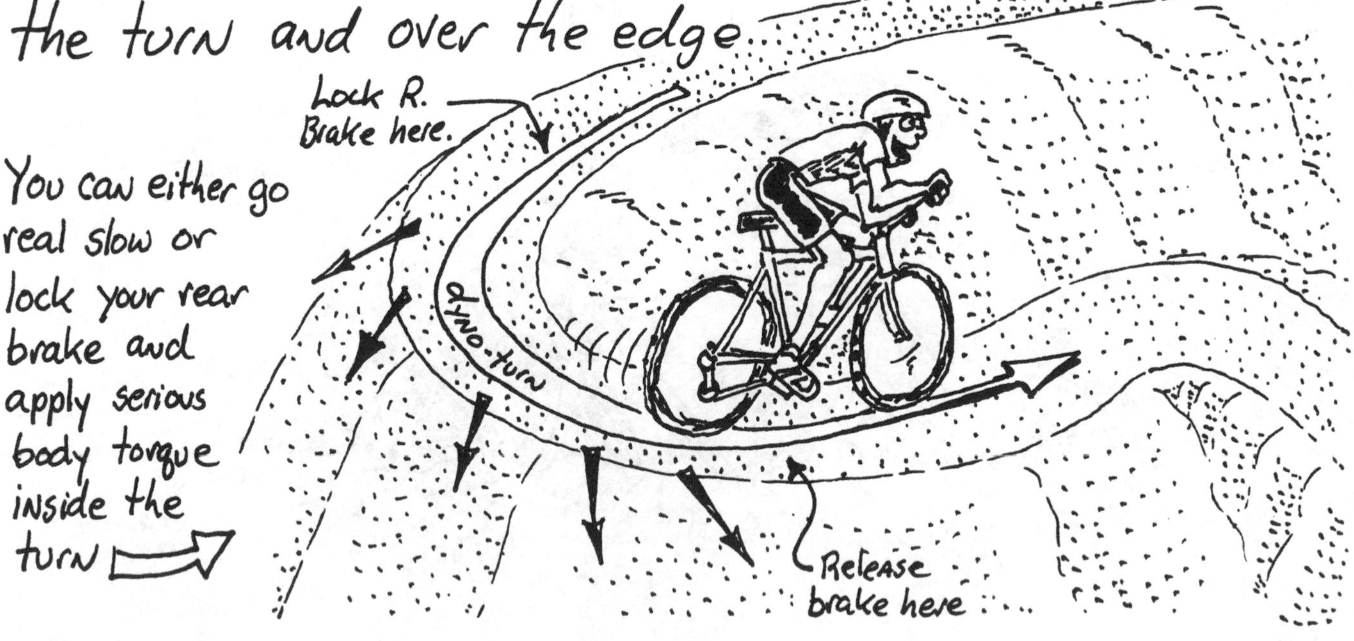

Lock R. Brake here.
You can either go real slow or lock your rear brake and apply serious body torque inside the turn
dyno-turn
Release brake here

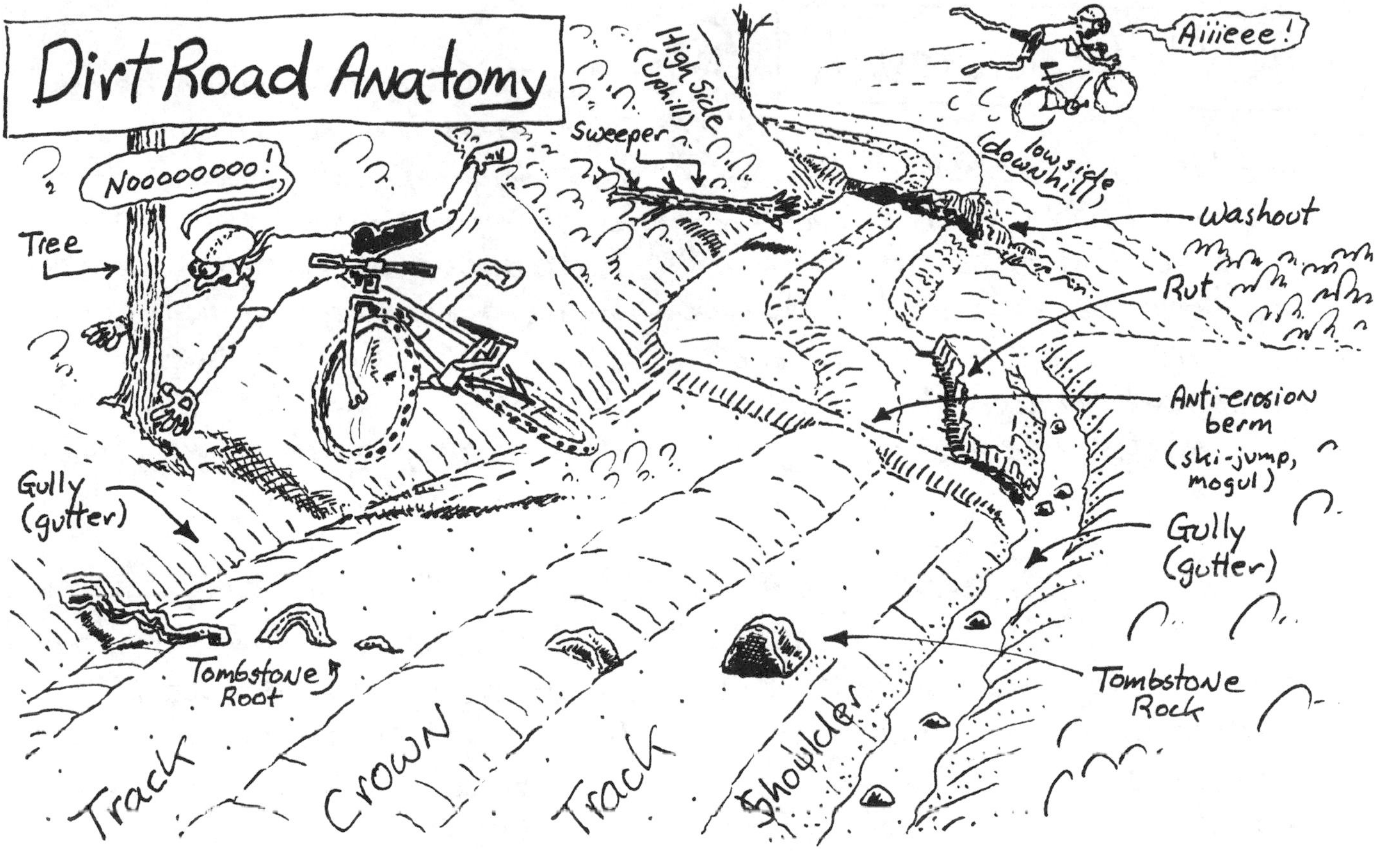
Dirt Road Anatomy
Nooooooo!
Tree
High Side (uphill)
Sweeper
Aiiieee!
low side (downhill)
Washout
Rut
Anti-erosion berm (ski-jump, mogul)
Gully (gutter)
Gully (gutter)
Tombstone Root
Tombstone Rock
Track
Crown
Track
Shoulder

Face Plant (fasê plânt) v., (A.k.a. "head dab," "head plant", "header", etc.) To abruptly establish initial ground contact with any portion of the head or face...

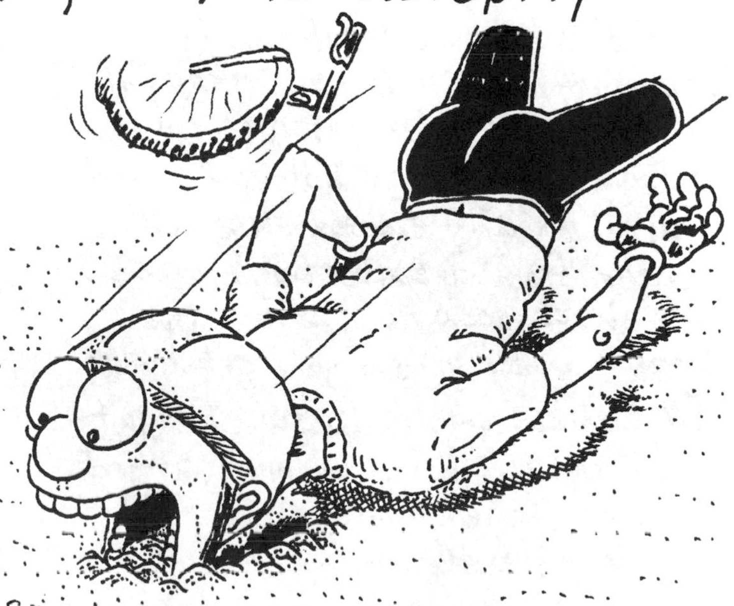

# Ask Dr. Conewrench

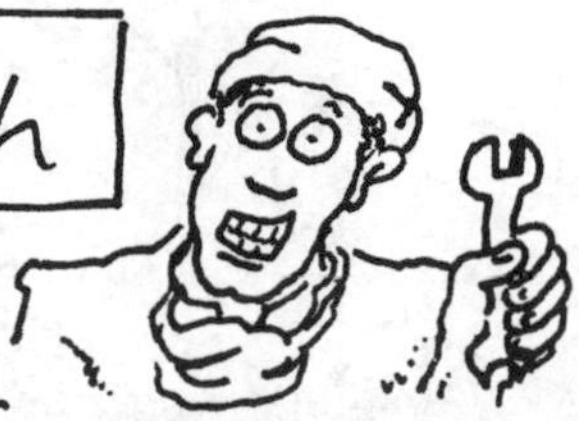

Dear Dr. Conewrench,

When I ride in the Summer I get a terrible case of scalp itch that even medicated shampoo won't cure. What is the name of this condition and has medical science developed a cure yet?

Tanya
Berkeley, CA.

Well, Tanya, you suffer from a rather common skin ailment we doctors call "Head Rot." Fortunately, there is a cure short of shaving your head and buffing it with a high-speed grinder. After a shampoo & rinse pour about half a cup of Listerine on your head & massage it into your scalp for 5 minutes then rinse. Blow dry if possible. [Editor's Note - Crazy as it sounds, this really works!]

Dear Dr. Conewrench,

I'm always riding thru patche of poison ivy in the woods. Is there any field treatment I should be doing to reduce my chances of breaking out? Also, do you know a good recipe for 'possum.

Bubba
Fort Payne, AL

The best field treatment for poison ivy/oak is to wash a.s.a.p. with soap & water. Chances are you won't actually have soap but you should still flush any exposed skin with water from a water bottle or a creek as soon as possible, then soap & water when you get home. Dr. Conewrench's Possum Delight; You'll need; 1 bottle wh. wine, 2 med. onions, sage, salt & pepper. First drink the bottle of wine. Stuff the dressed 'possum with onions, rub with sage, salt, and pepper. Bake in oven for 20 minutes per pound (about 2 hrs. for a good-size one). After baking, bury the 'possum in the backyard, feed the onions to the dogs & get someone to drive you to McDonalds for dinner.

Dear Dr. Conewrench,

What is the best treatment for a guy who strikes his private parts on the seat while hopping a log?

Vanna
Los Angeles, CA

Dear Vanna,

Quick painless euthanasia.

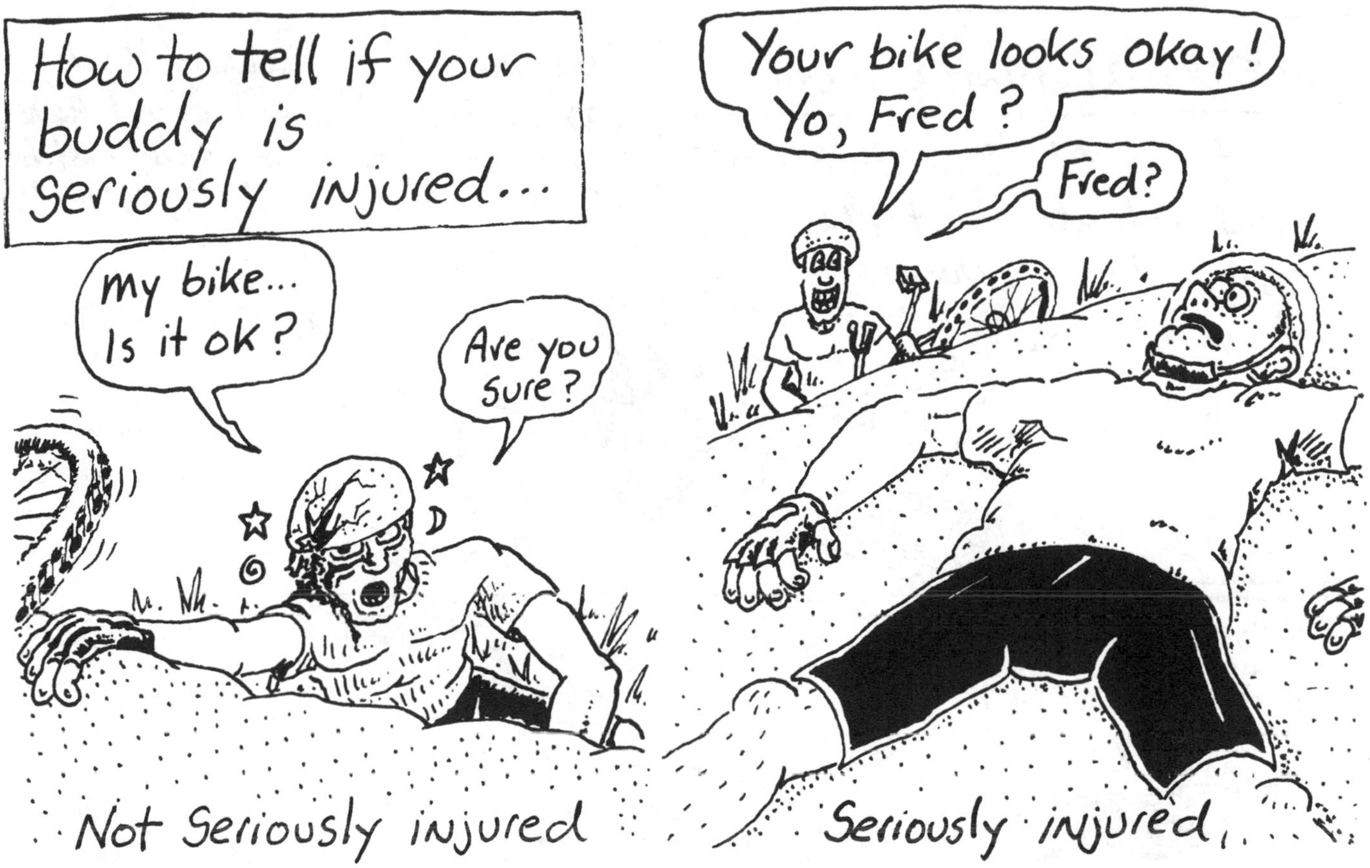
How to tell if your buddy is seriously injured...
my bike... Is it ok?
Are you sure?
Not Seriously injured
Your bike looks okay! Yo, Fred?
Fred?
Seriously injured.

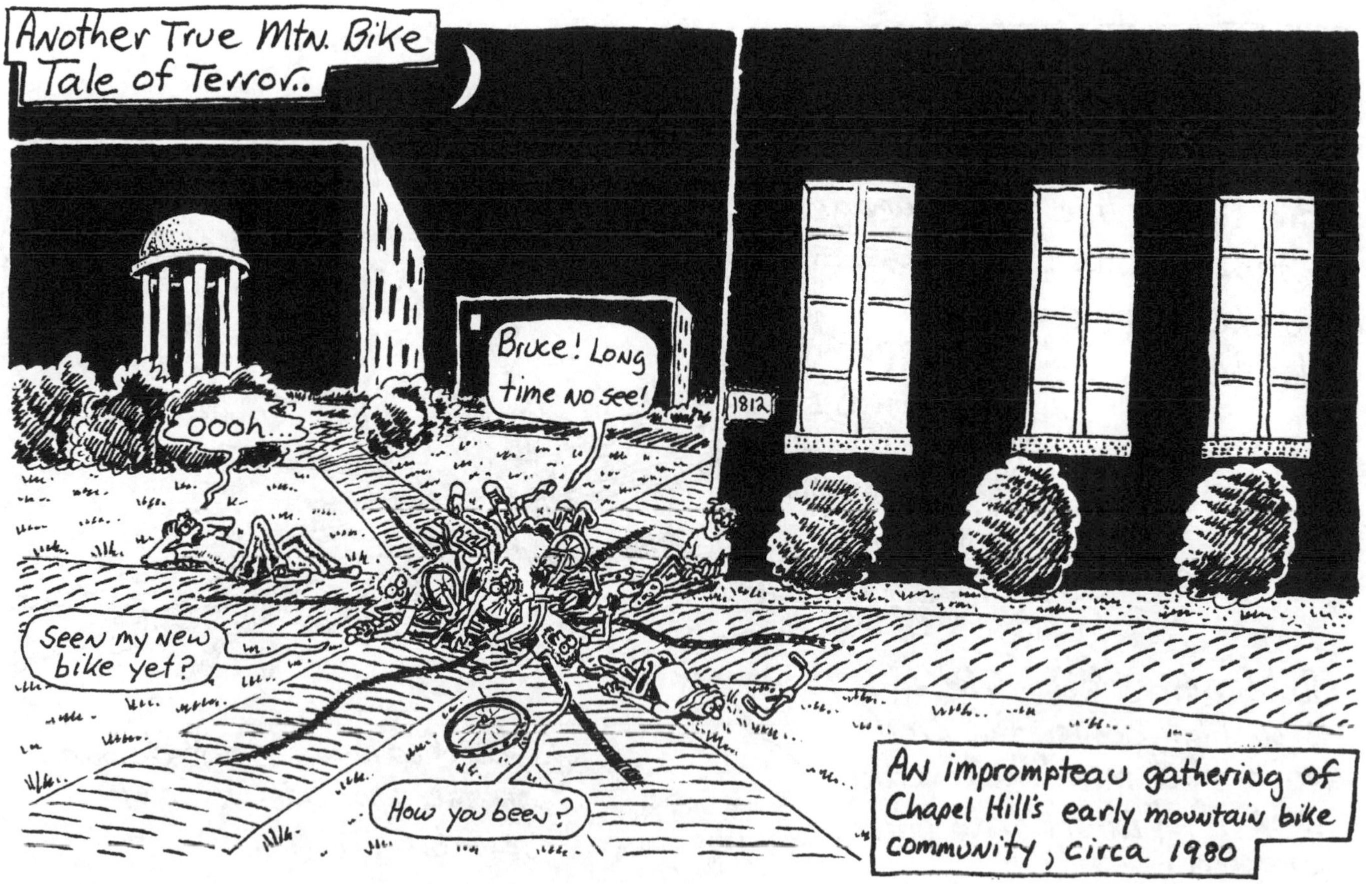
Another True Mtn. Bike Tale of Terror..
Bruce! Long time no see!
1812
oooh...
Seen my new bike yet?
How you been?
An imprompteau gathering of Chapel Hill's early mountain bike community, circa 1980

# Unethical Trail Grooming

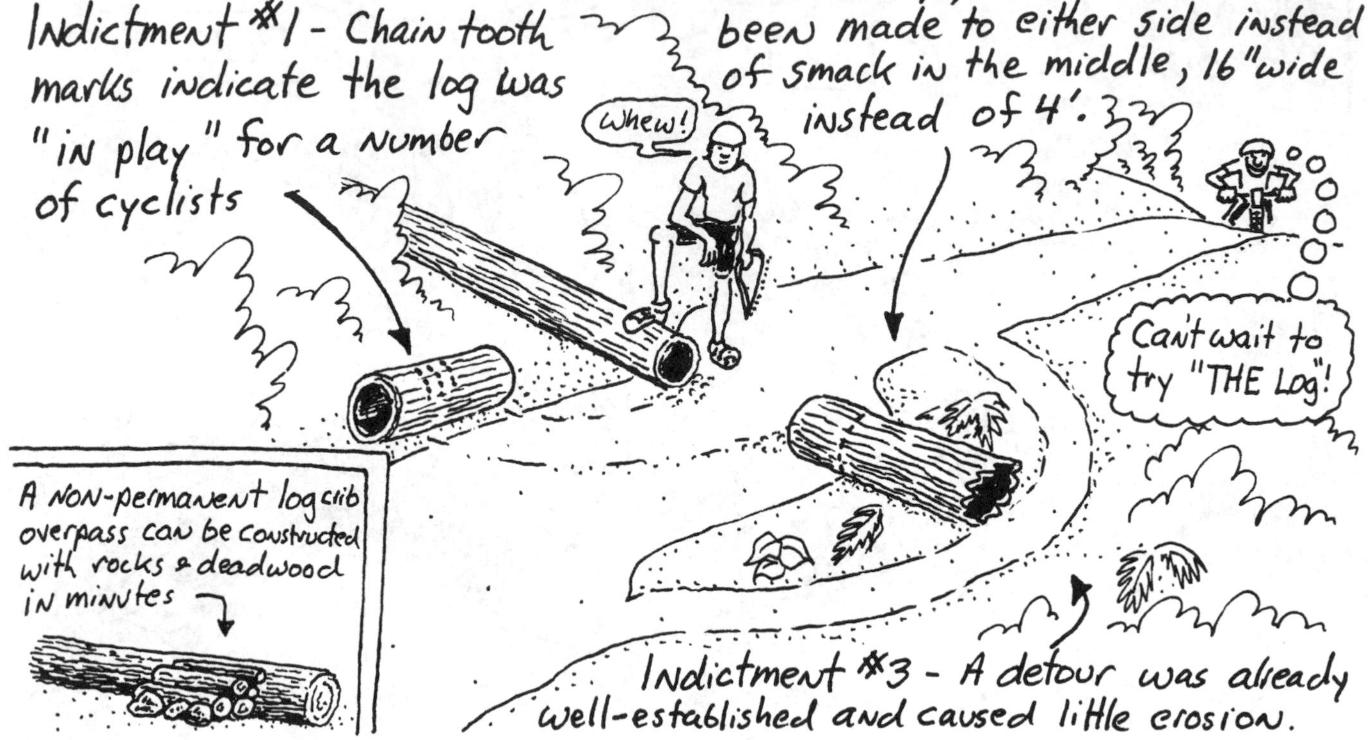
Indictment #1 - Chain tooth marks indicate the log was "in play" for a number of cyclists
Whew!
Indictment #2 - Knowing the log was "in play", the cut could have been made to either side instead of smack in the middle, 16" wide instead of 4'.
Can't wait to try "THE Log"!
A NON-permanent log crib overpass can be constructed with rocks & deadwood in minutes
Indictment #3 - A detour was already well-established and caused little erosion.

# Ethical Trail Grooming

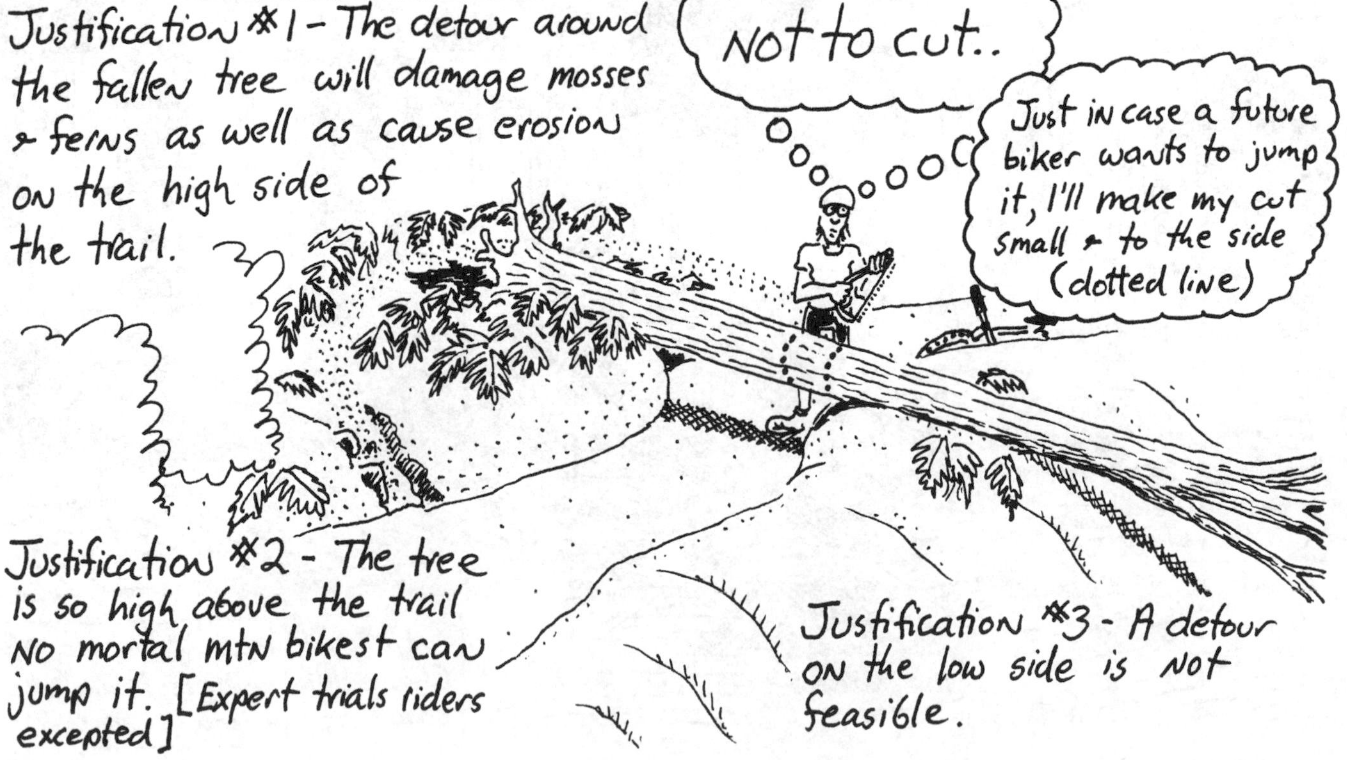
Justification #1 - The detour around the fallen tree will damage mosses & ferns as well as cause erosion on the high side of the trail.
To cut or not to cut..
Just in case a future biker wants to jump it, I'll make my cut small & to the side (dotted line)
Justification #2 - The tree is so high above the trail no mortal mtn bikest can jump it. [Expert trials riders excepted]
Justification #3 - A detour on the low side is not feasible.

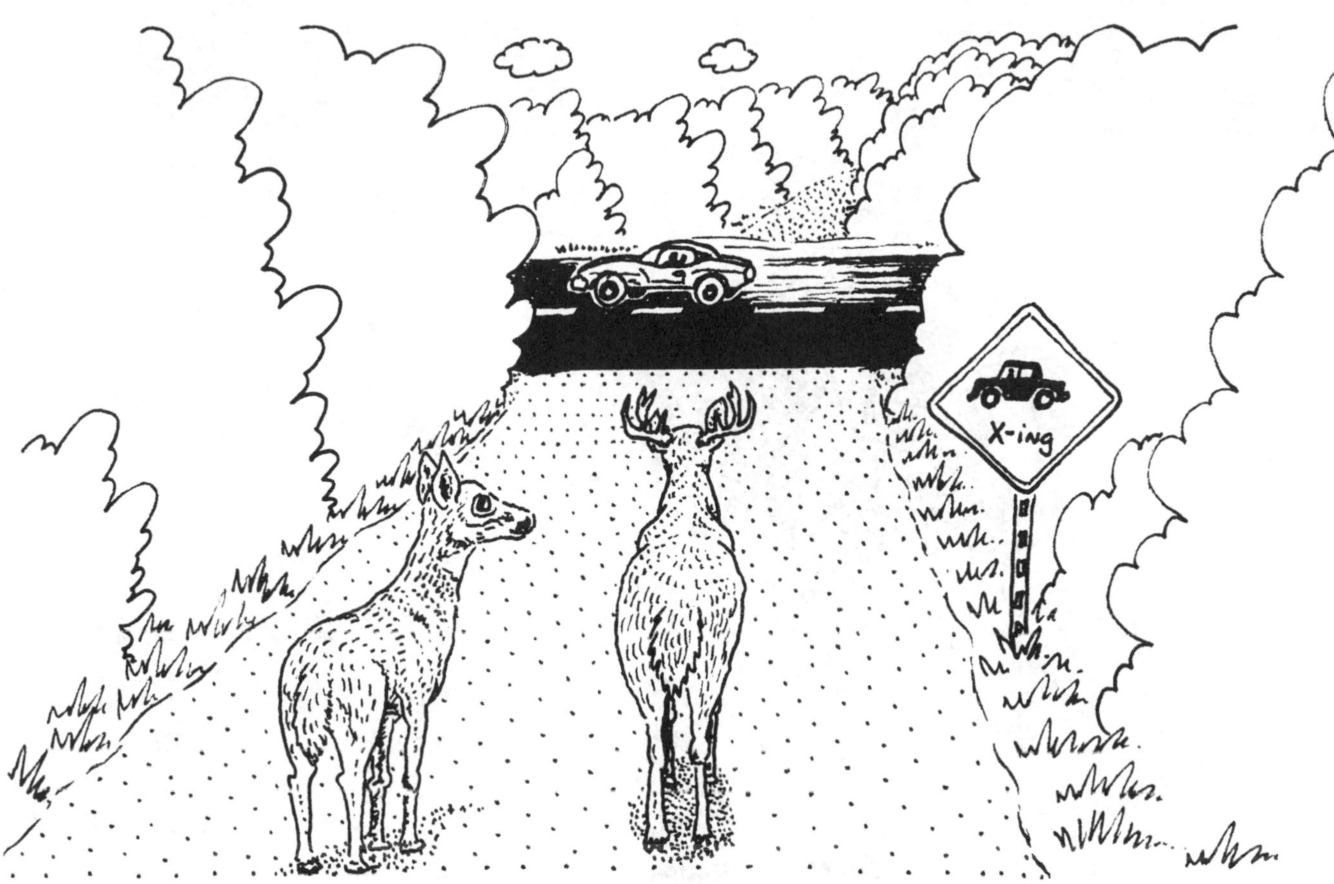
X-ing

Humor concept by H. Wallace

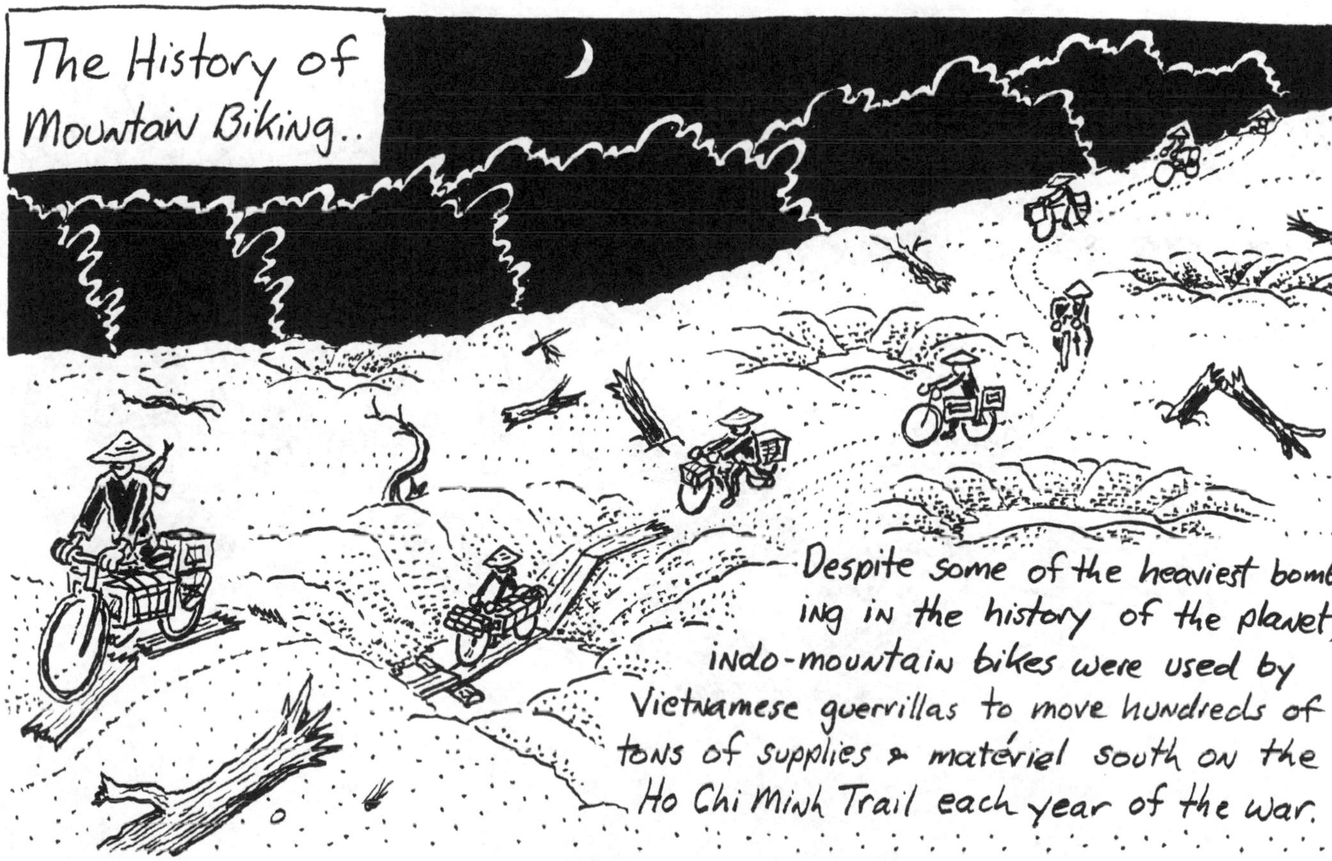
The History of Mountain Biking..
Despite some of the heaviest bombing in the history of the planet, indo-mountain bikes were used by Vietnamese guerrillas to move hundreds of tons of supplies & matériel south on the Ho Chi Minh Trail each year of the war.

## Bad Habit #17

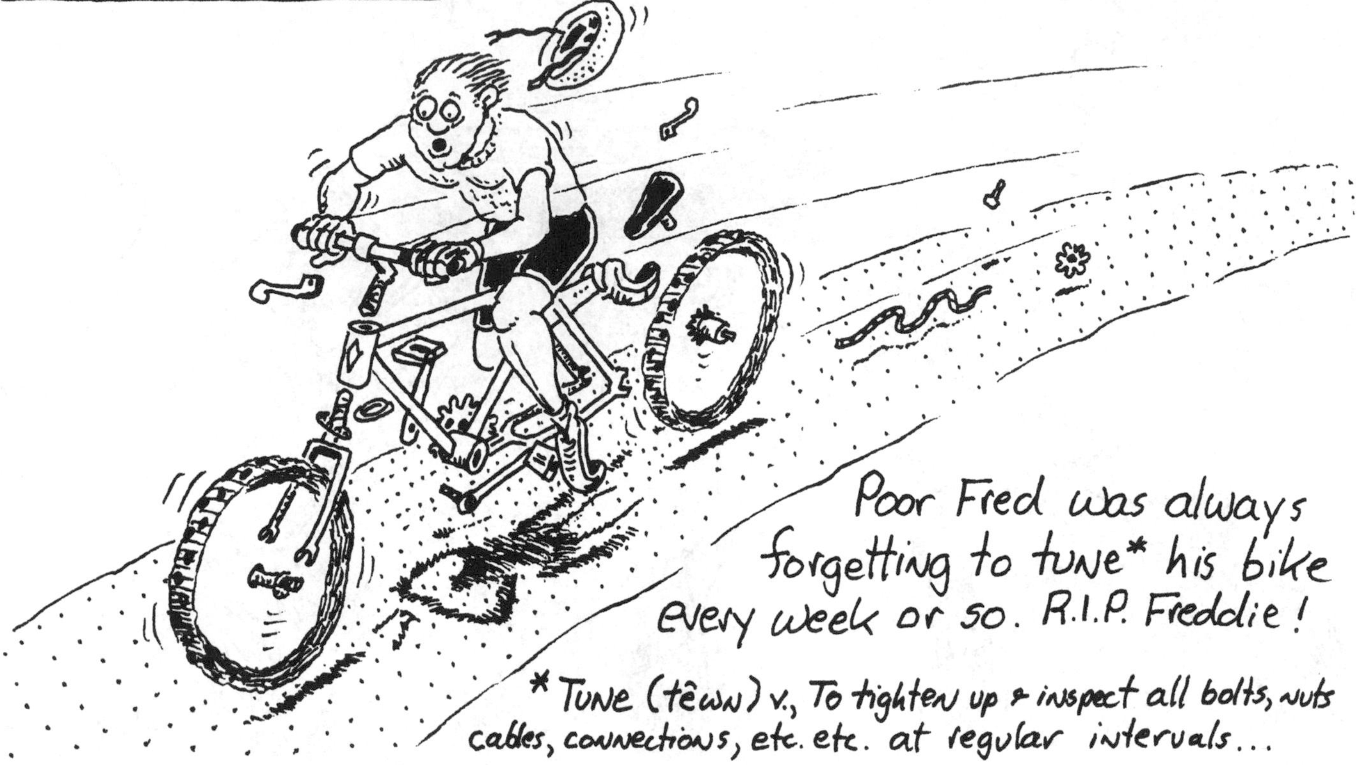

Poor Fred was always forgetting to tune* his bike every week or so. R.I.P. Freddie!

* Tune (têwn) v., To tighten up & inspect all bolts, nuts cables, connections, etc. etc. at regular intervals...

Body Carve (bôd·ē carv) v., (Aka. "Body Slam" etc.) To dynamically come off your bike and do some trenching with your torso...

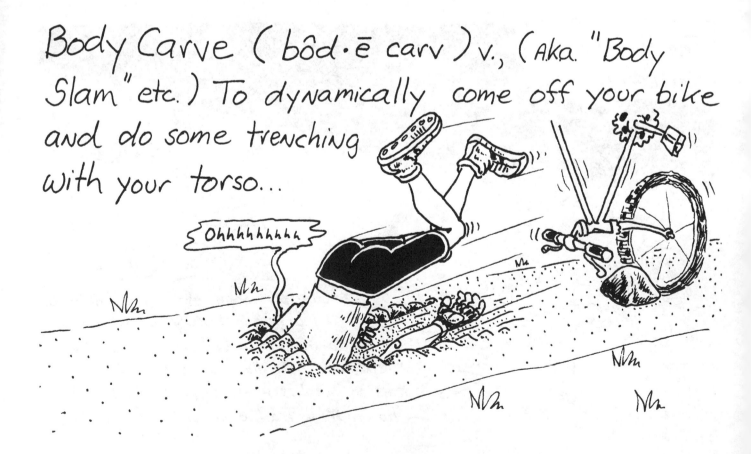

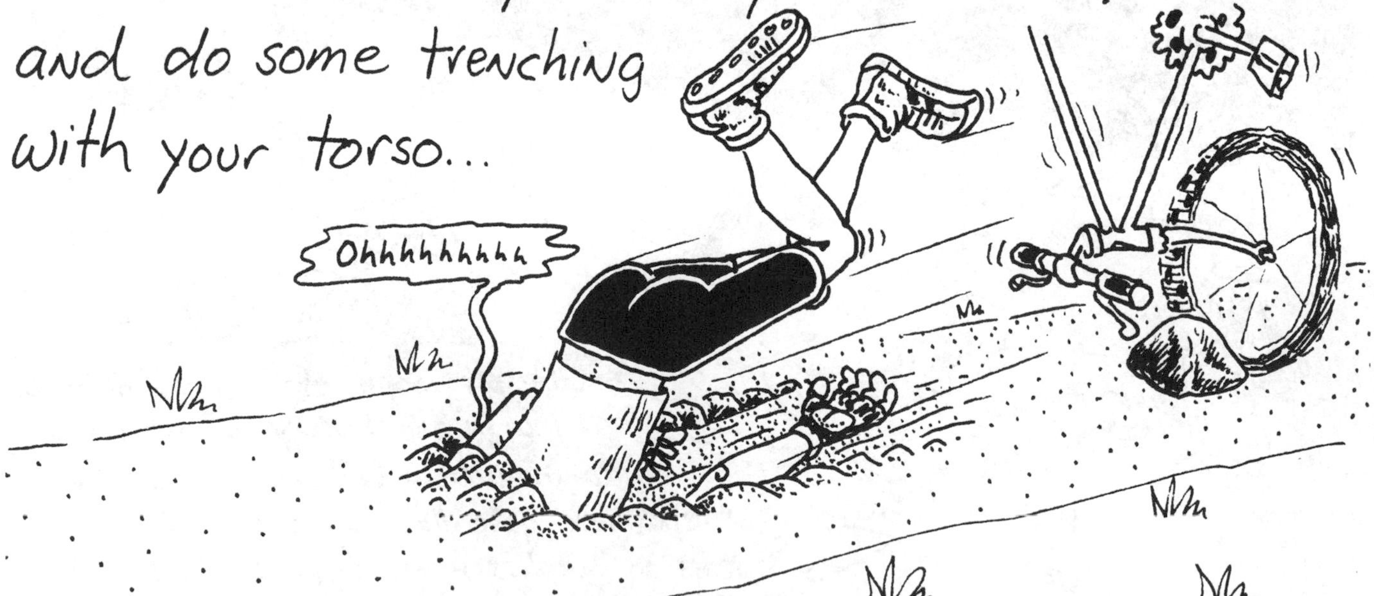
Ohhhhhhhhh

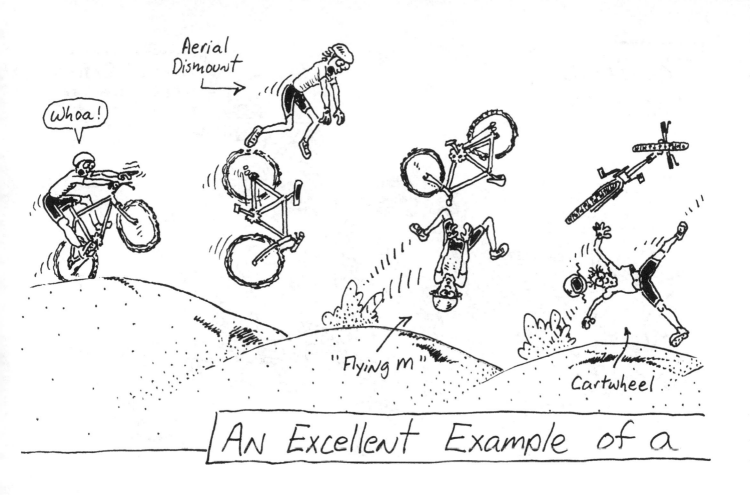

Whoa!
Aerial Dismount
"Flying M"
Cartwheel
An Excellent Example of a
Cartwheel, contd.
T-bone
Full Pike Front Flip
Probably not seriously injured
...my bike...
Super-dynamic Crash and Burn

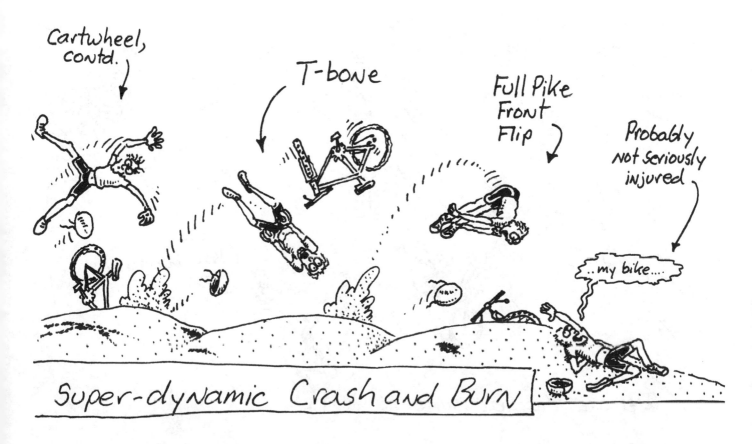

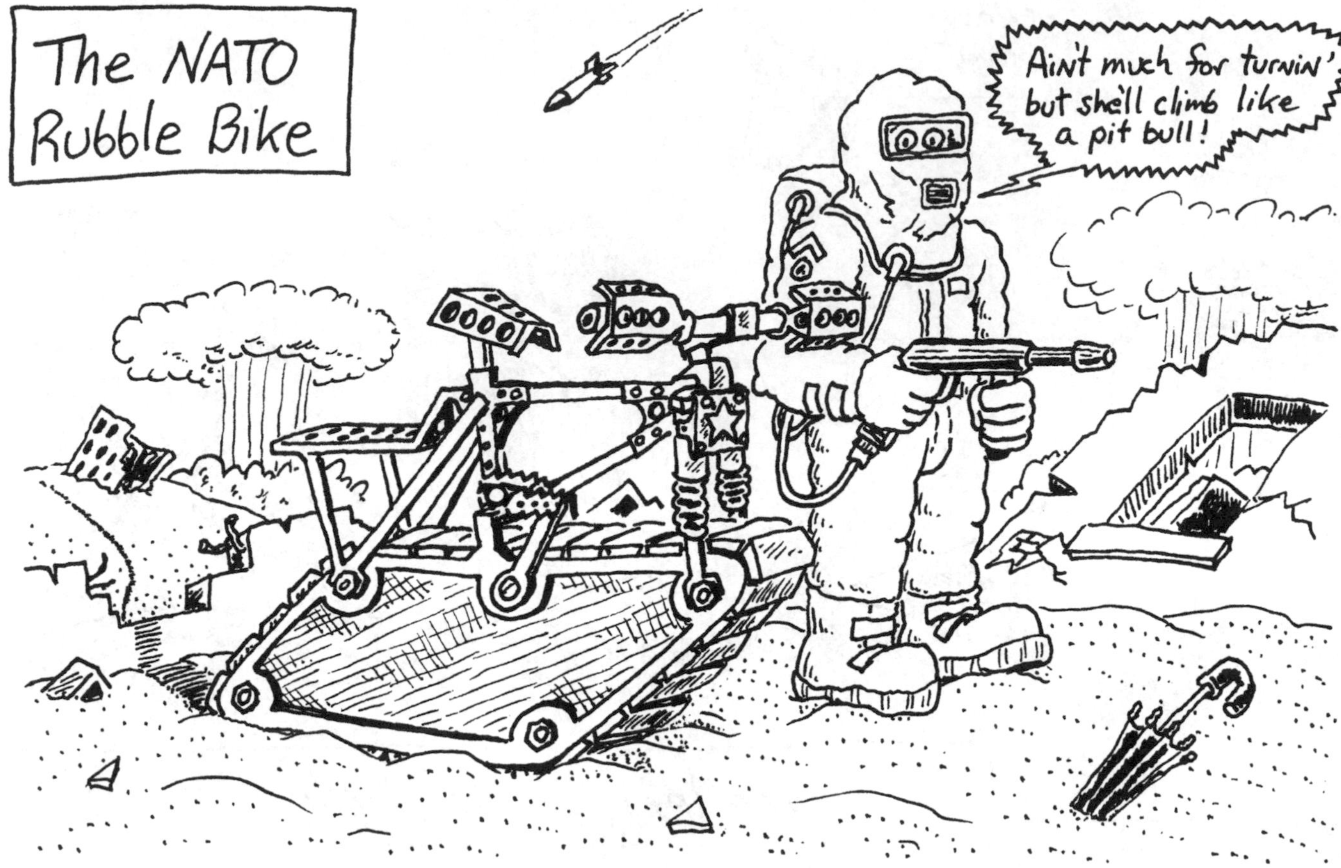
The NATO Rubble Bike
Ain't much for turnin' but she'll climb like a pit bull!

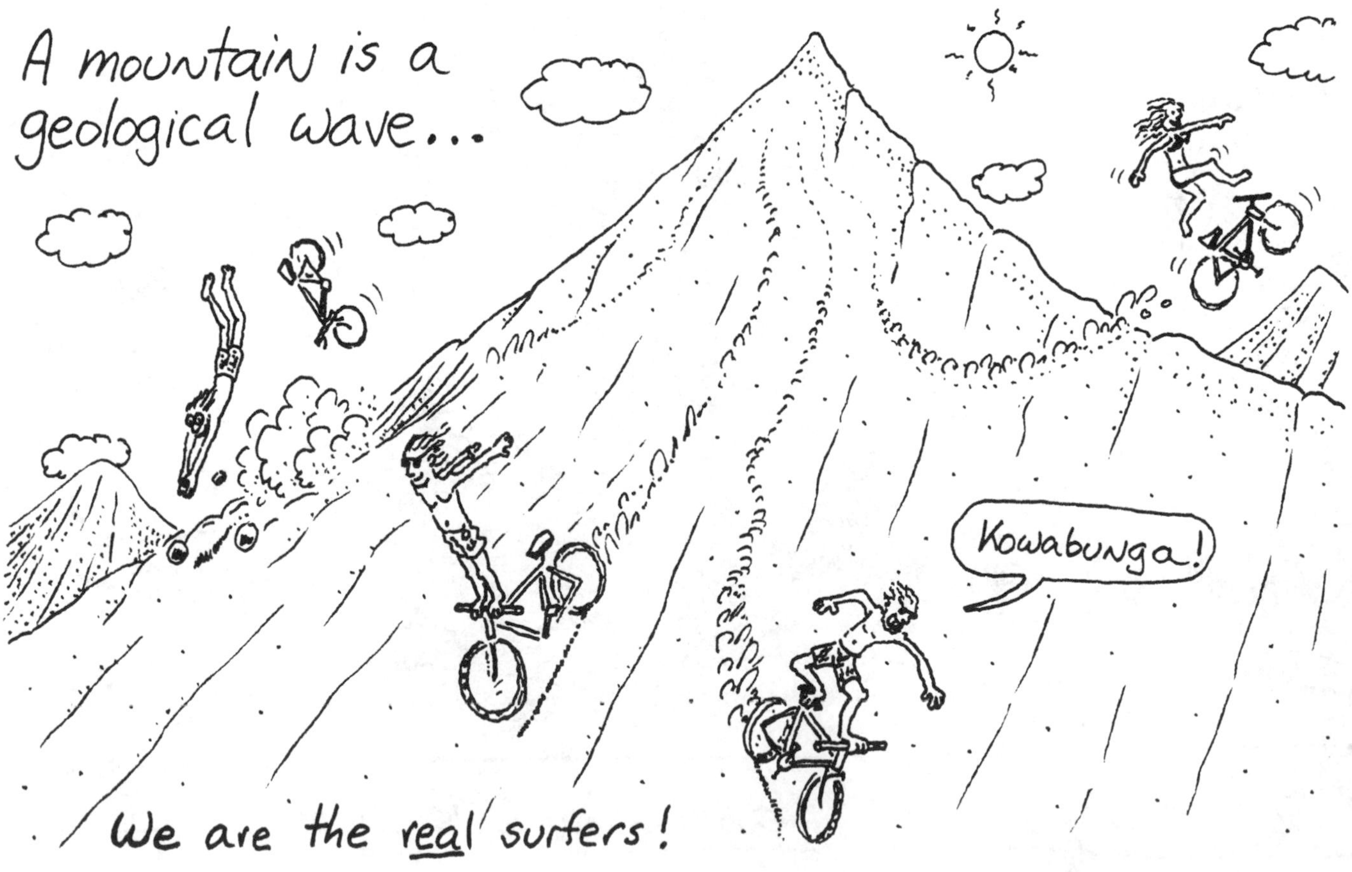
A mountain is a geological wave...
Kowabunga!
We are the real surfers!

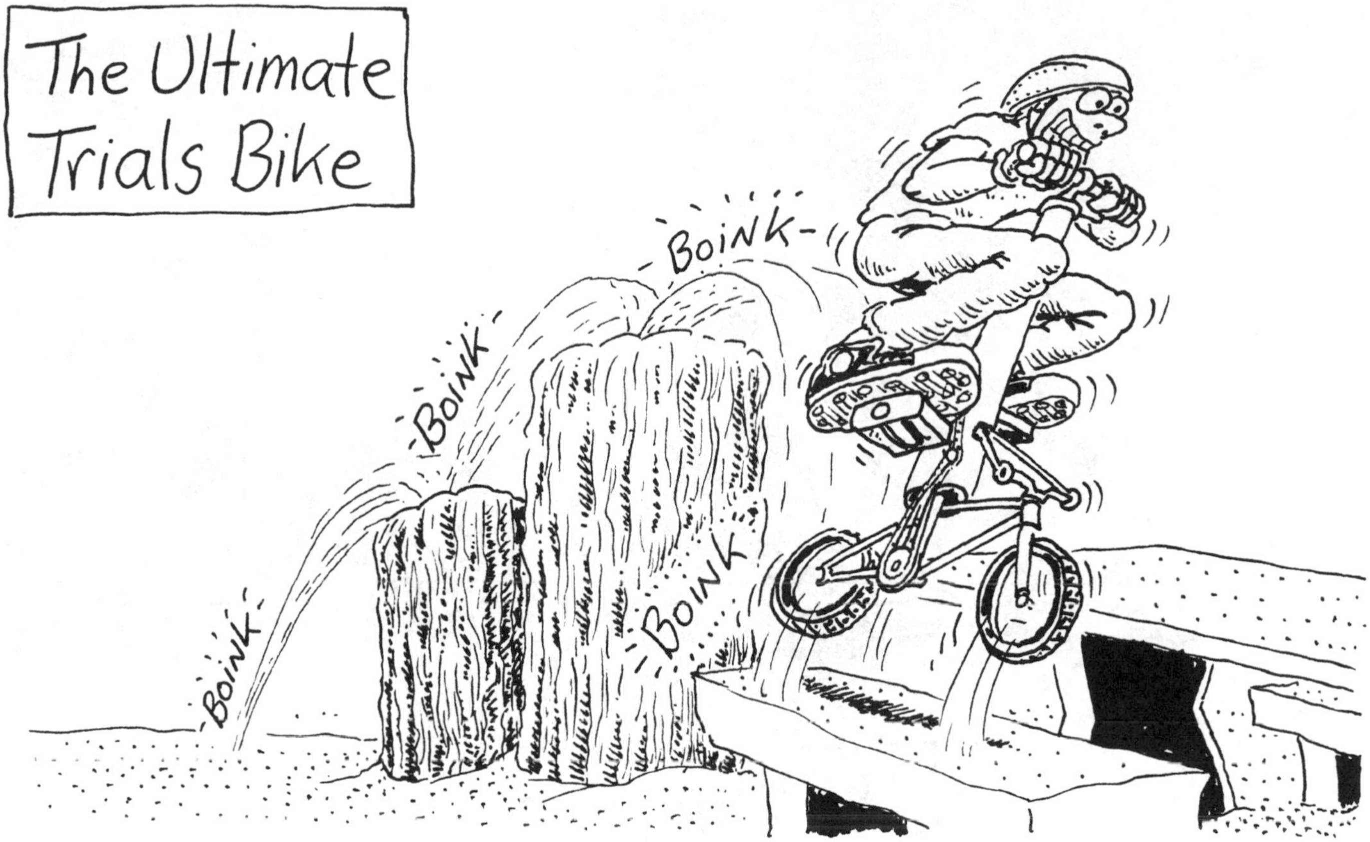
BOINK
BOINK
BOINK
BOINK
BOINK
The Ultimate Trials Bike

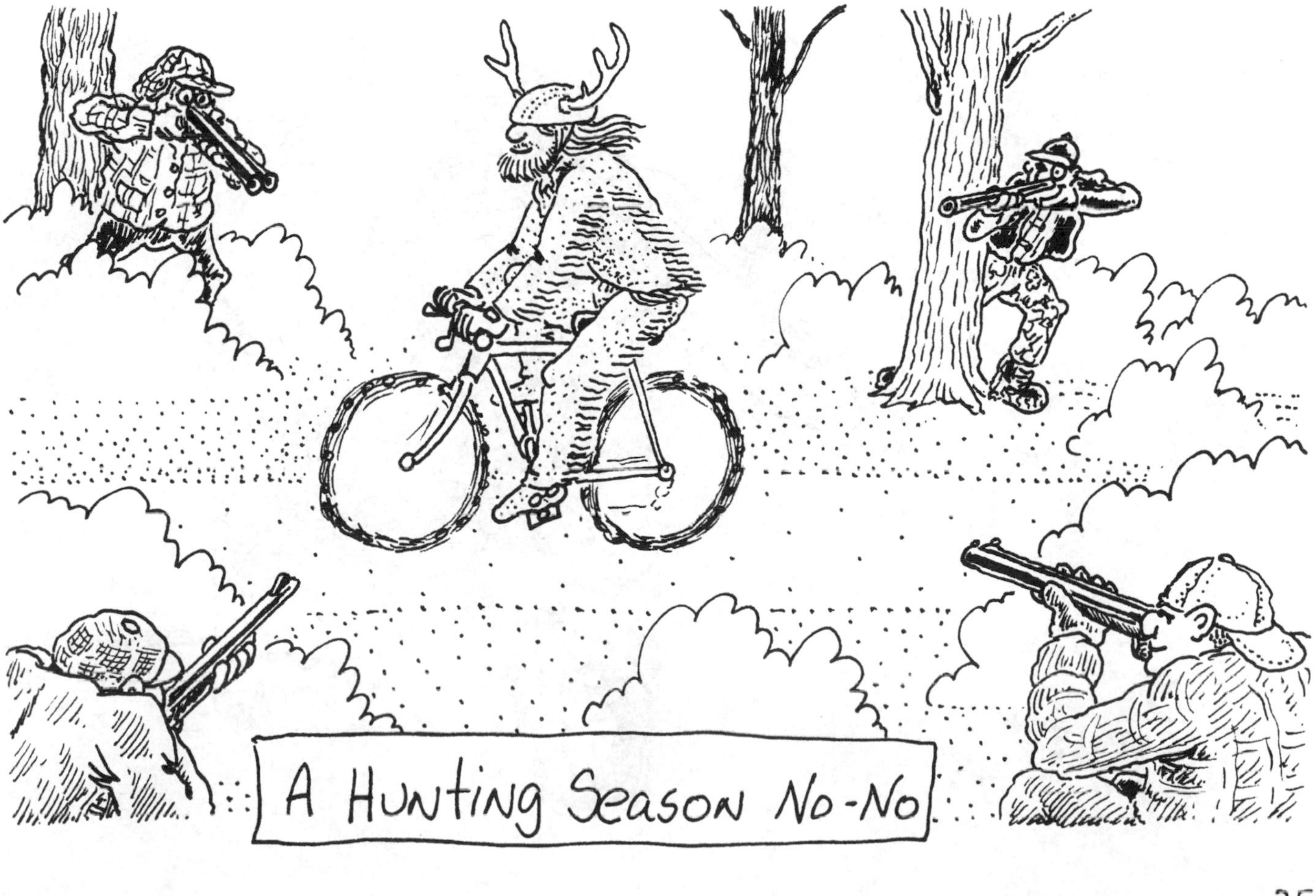
A Hunting Season No-No

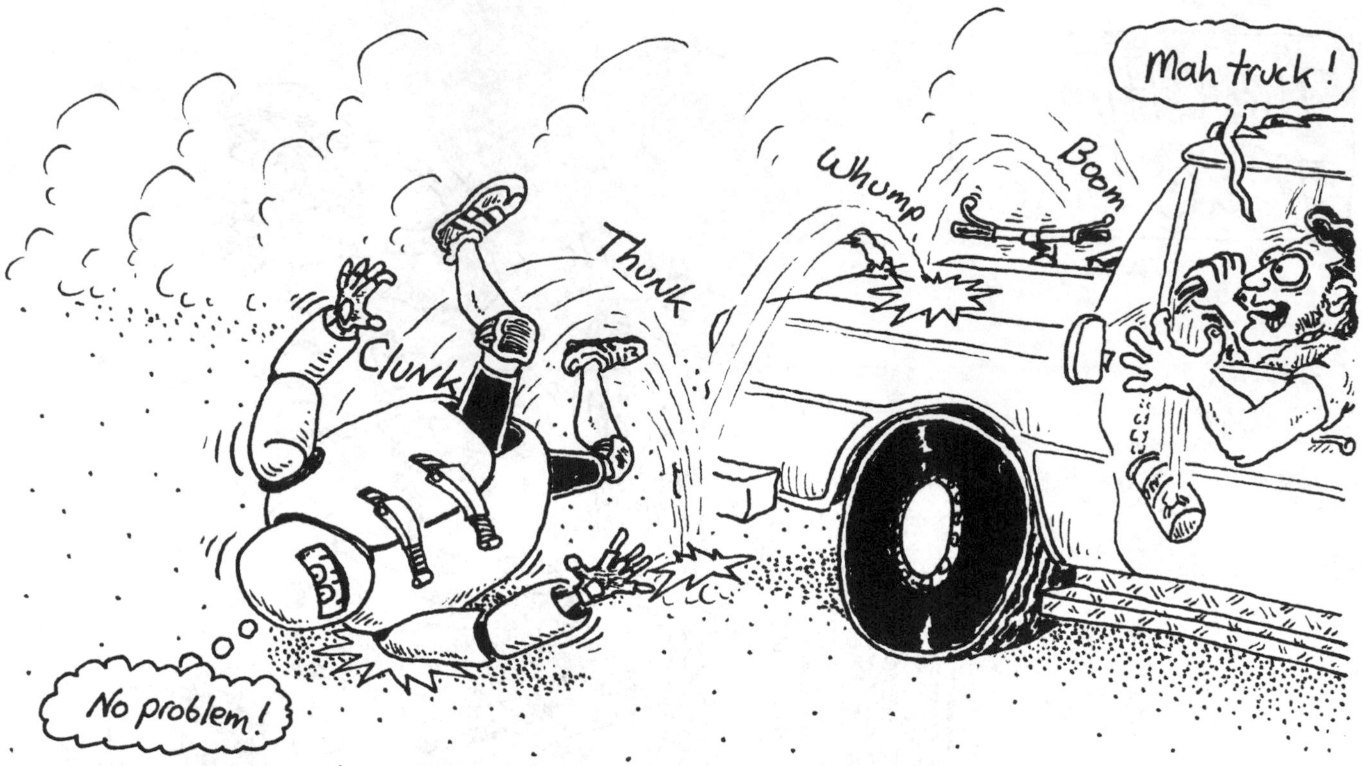
Mah truck!
Whump
Boom
Thunk
Clunk
No problem!

The Body Helmet

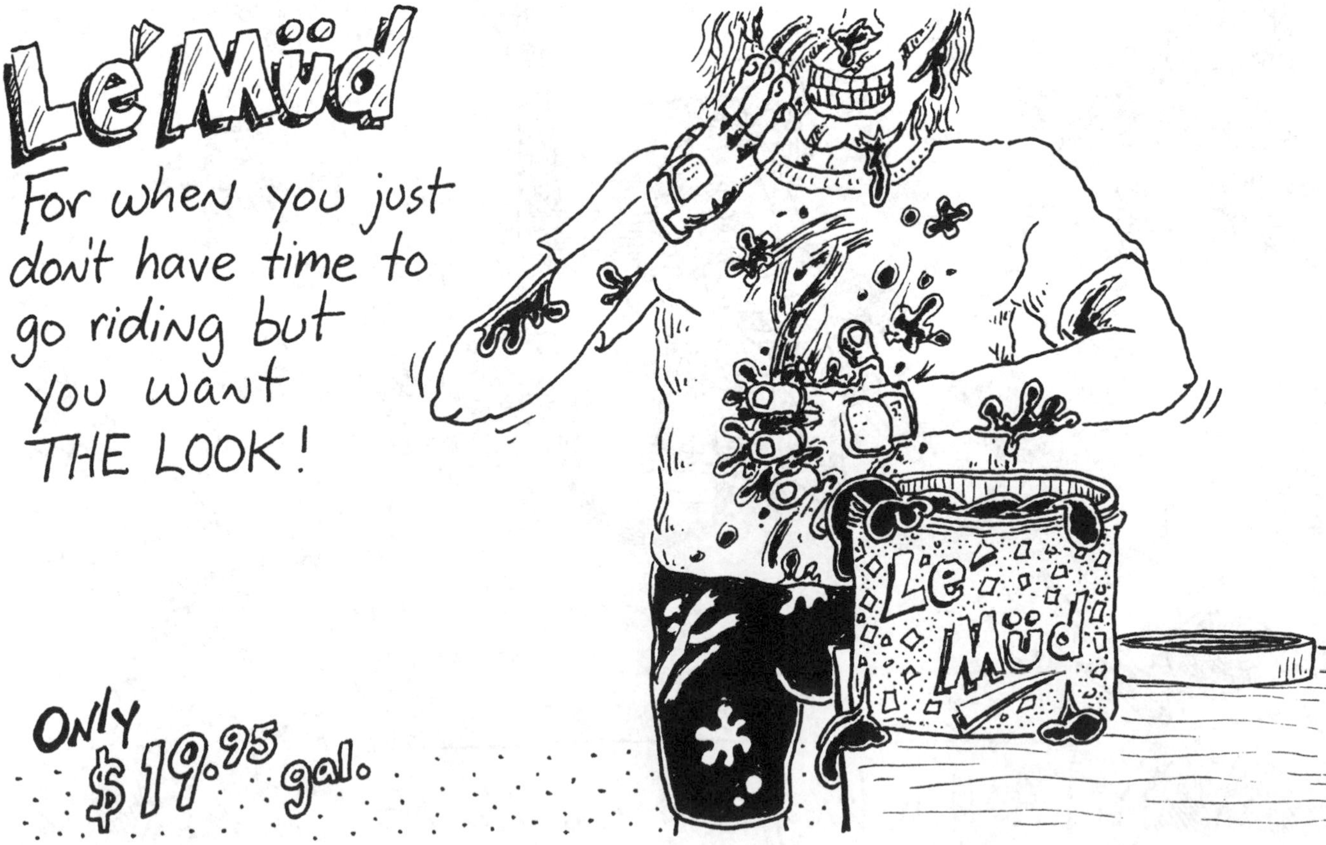
Lé Müd
For when you just don't have time to go riding but you want THE LOOK!
Only $19.95 gal.
Lé Müd

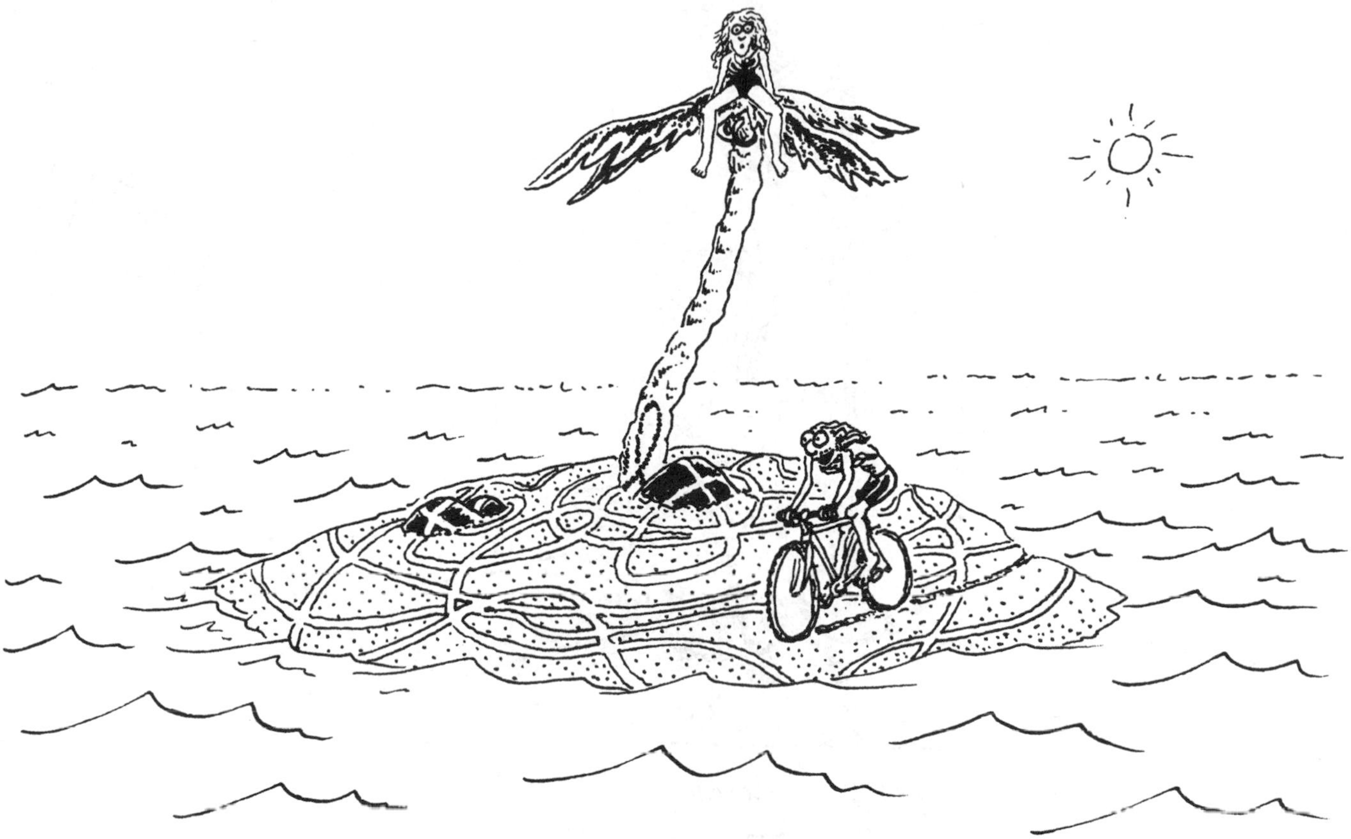

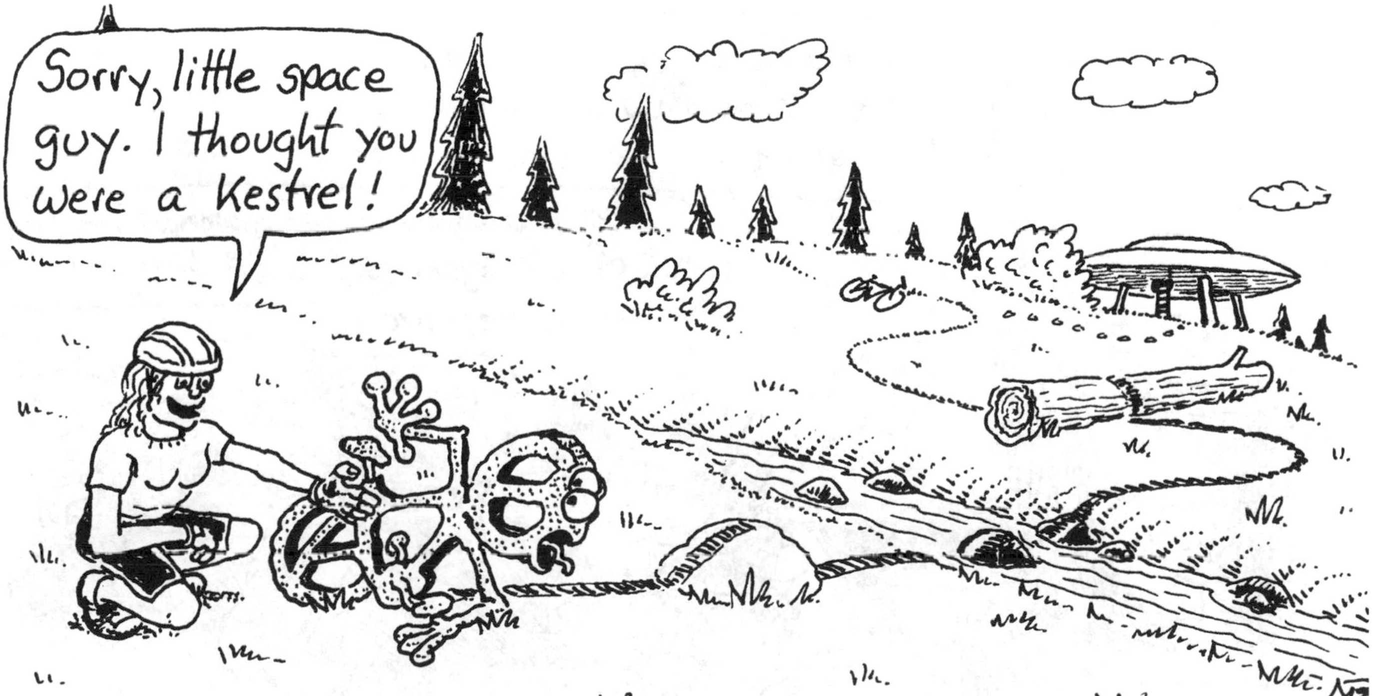
Sorry, little space guy. I thought you were a Kestrel!

Close Encounters of the 4th Kind

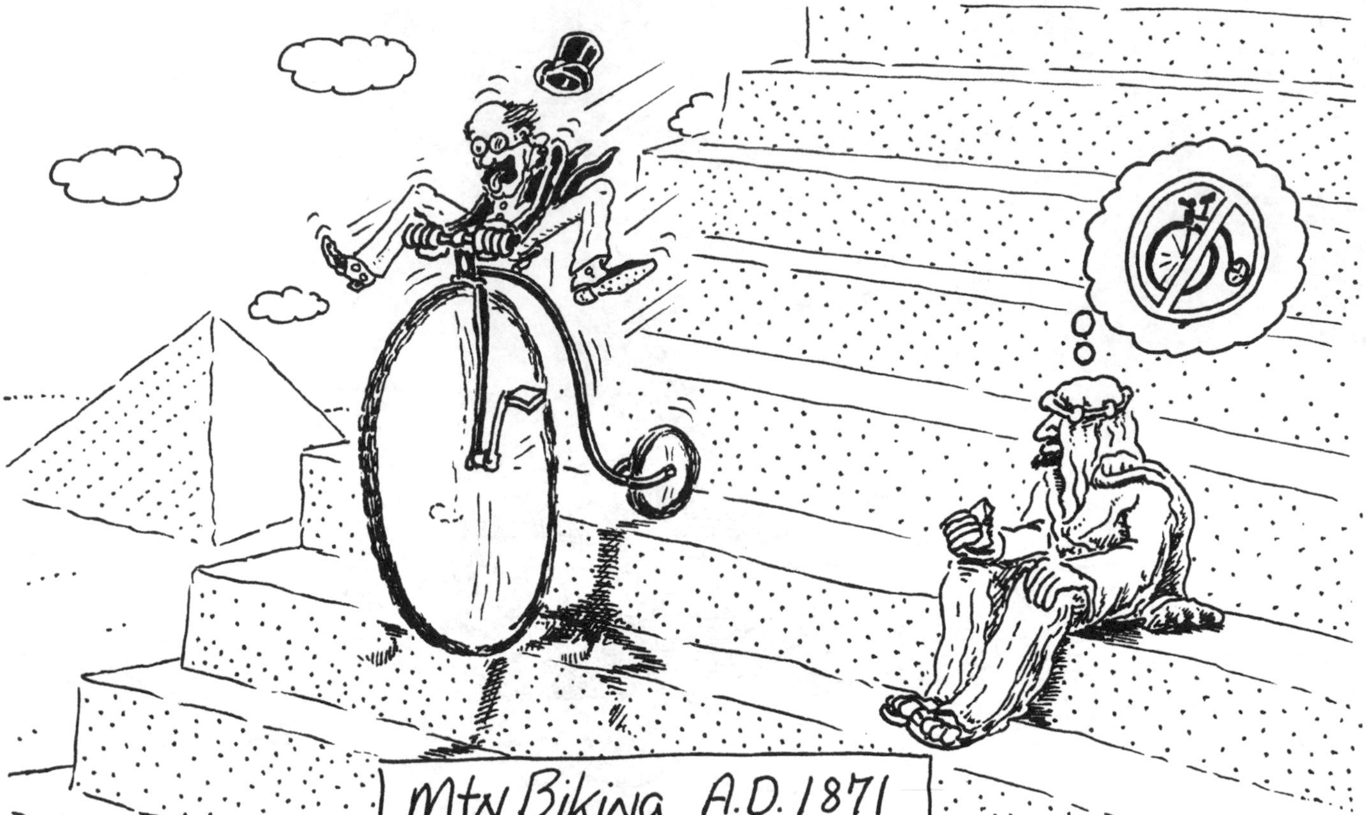

Mtn Biking A.D. 1871

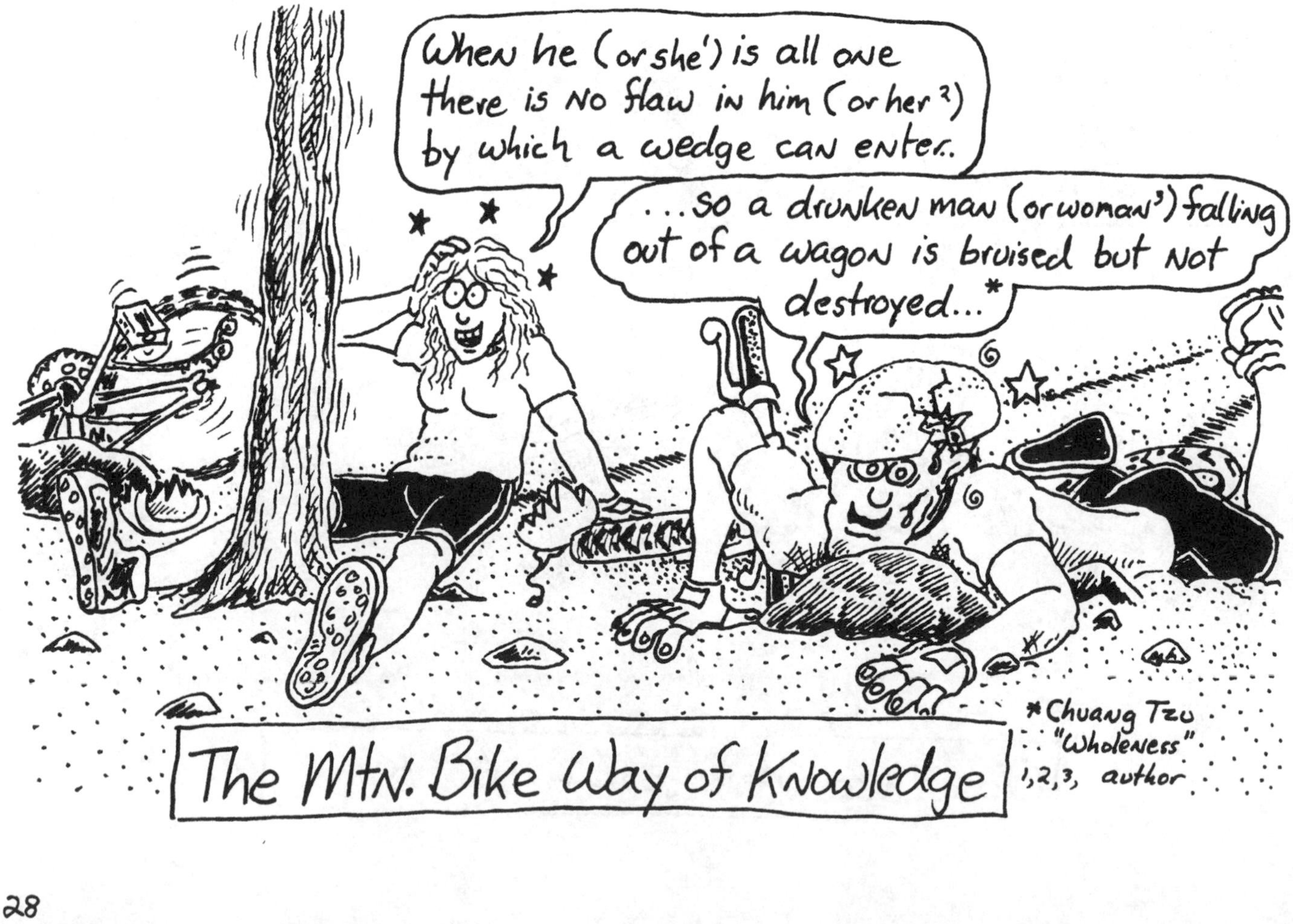
When he (or she[1]) is all one there is no flaw in him (or her[2]) by which a wedge can enter.
...so a drunken man (or woman[3]) falling out of a wagon is bruised but not destroyed...*
*Chuang Tzu "Wholeness"
1,2,3, author

The Mtn. Bike Way of Knowledge

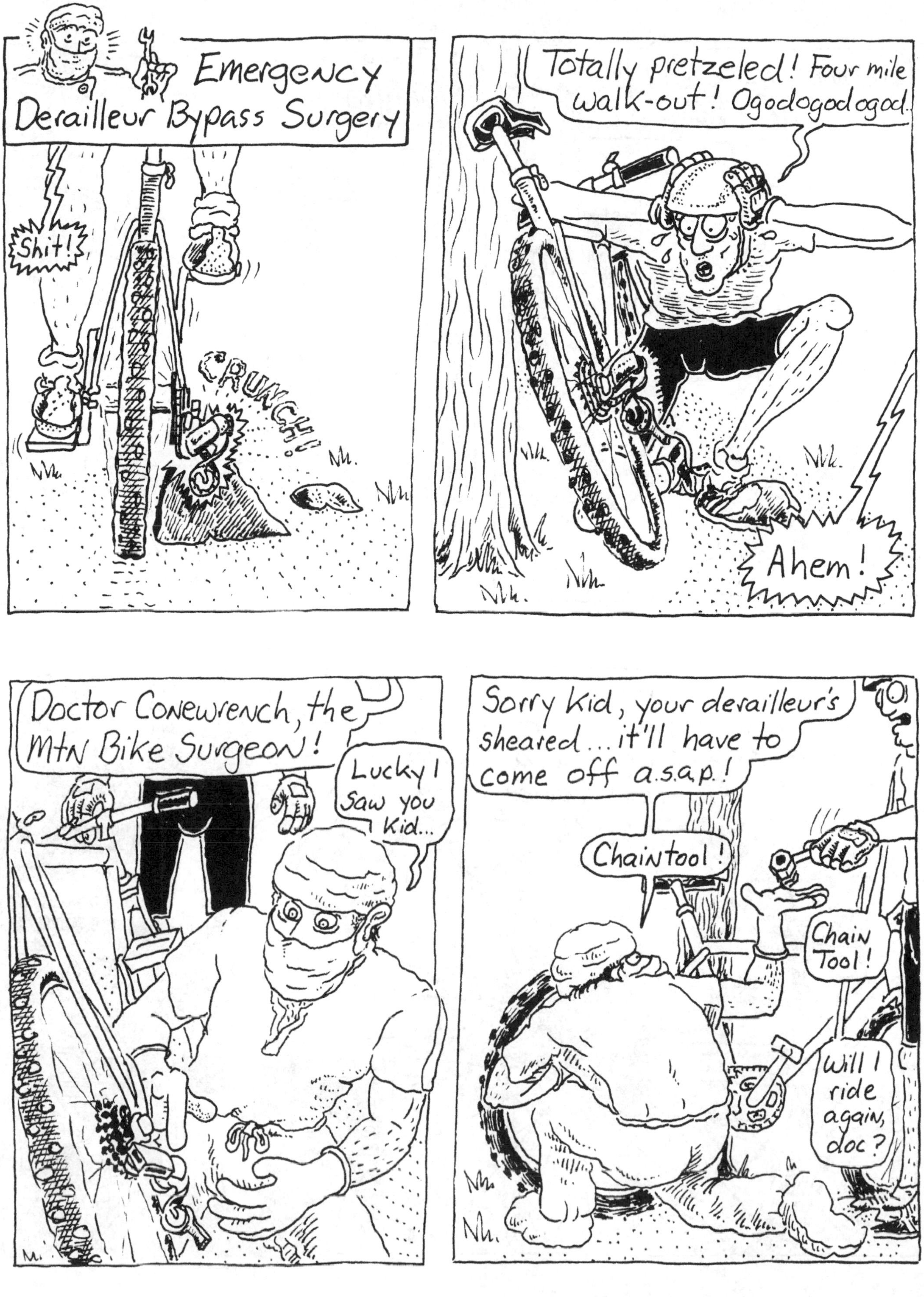
Emergency Derailleur Bypass Surgery
Shit!
CRUNCH!!
Totally pretzeled! Four mile walk-out! Ogodogodogod.
Ahem!
Doctor Conewrench, the Mtn Bike Surgeon!
Lucky! Saw you Kid...
Sorry Kid, your derailleur's sheared... it'll have to come off a.s.a.p.!
Chaintool!
Chain Tool!
Will I ride again, doc?

15 mm wrench!
15 mm wrench.
There, it's off... Nice paper-weight...
Sponge!
Sponge.
Now, we remove some links, put your chain on your lowest gear, align the tire and voila'.. No walking for you today!
Wow!
Be cool, Kid!
heh heh
Thanks, Dr. Cavewrench!
Later
Damn! He got my tool kit..

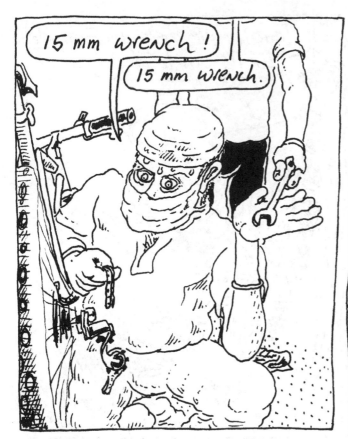

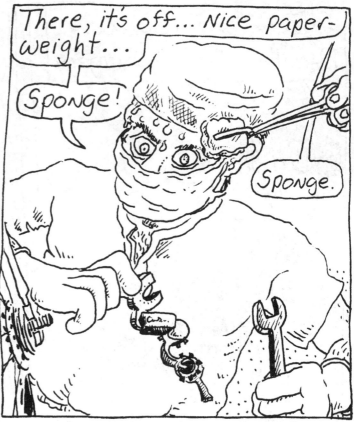

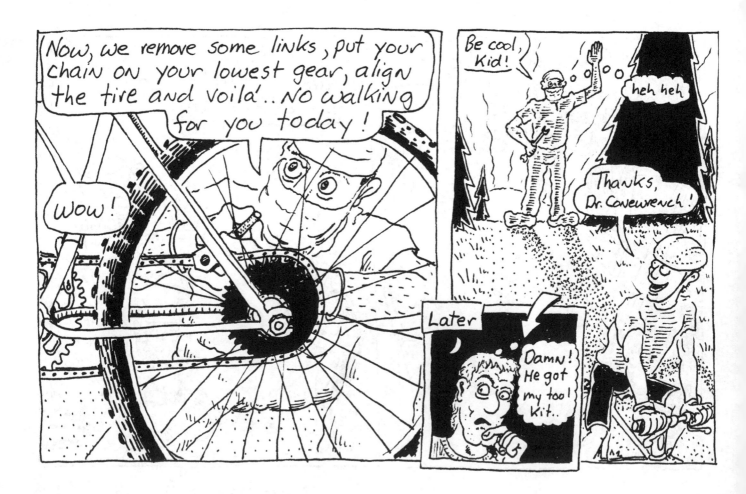

# All about Head Angle

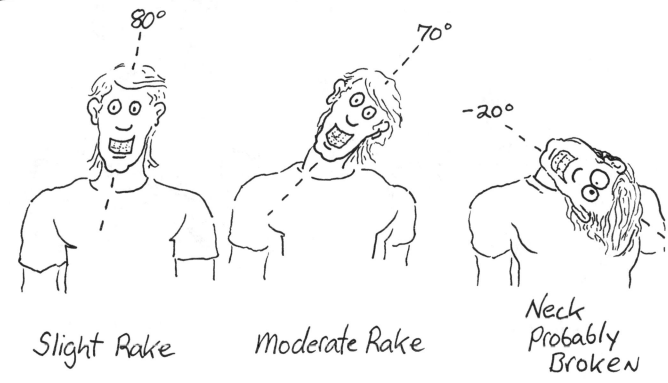

80°

Slight Rake

70°

Moderate Rake

-20°

Neck Probably Broken

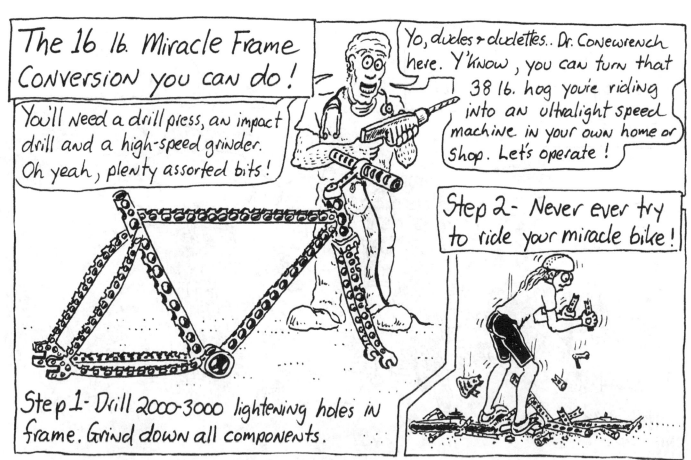

## The 16 lb. Miracle Frame Conversion you can do!

You'll need a drill press, an impact drill and a high-speed grinder. Oh yeah, plenty assorted bits!

Yo, dudes & dudettes.. Dr. Conewrench here. Y'know, you can turn that 38 lb. hog you're riding into an ultralight speed machine in your own home or shop. Let's operate!

Step 1 - Drill 2000-3000 lightening holes in frame. Grind down all components.

Step 2 - Never ever try to ride your miracle bike!

All about Seat Height

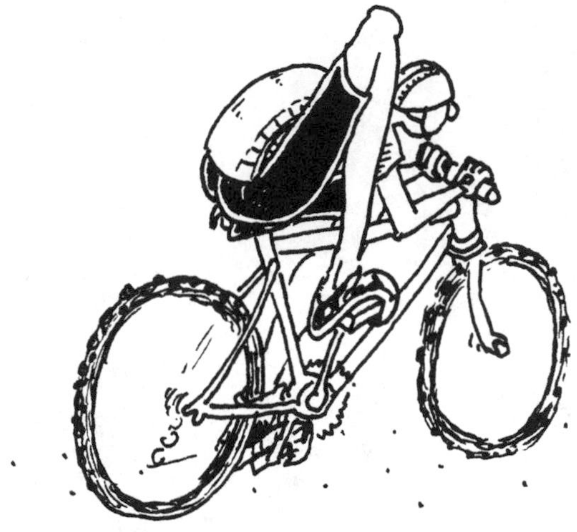

Seat too low

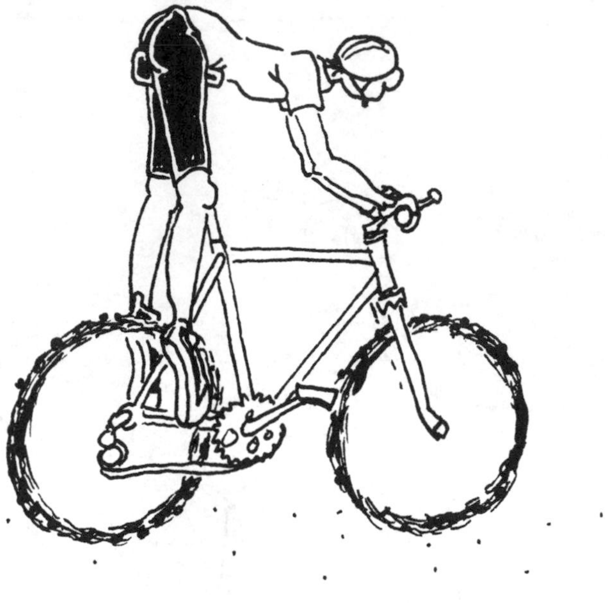

Seat too high

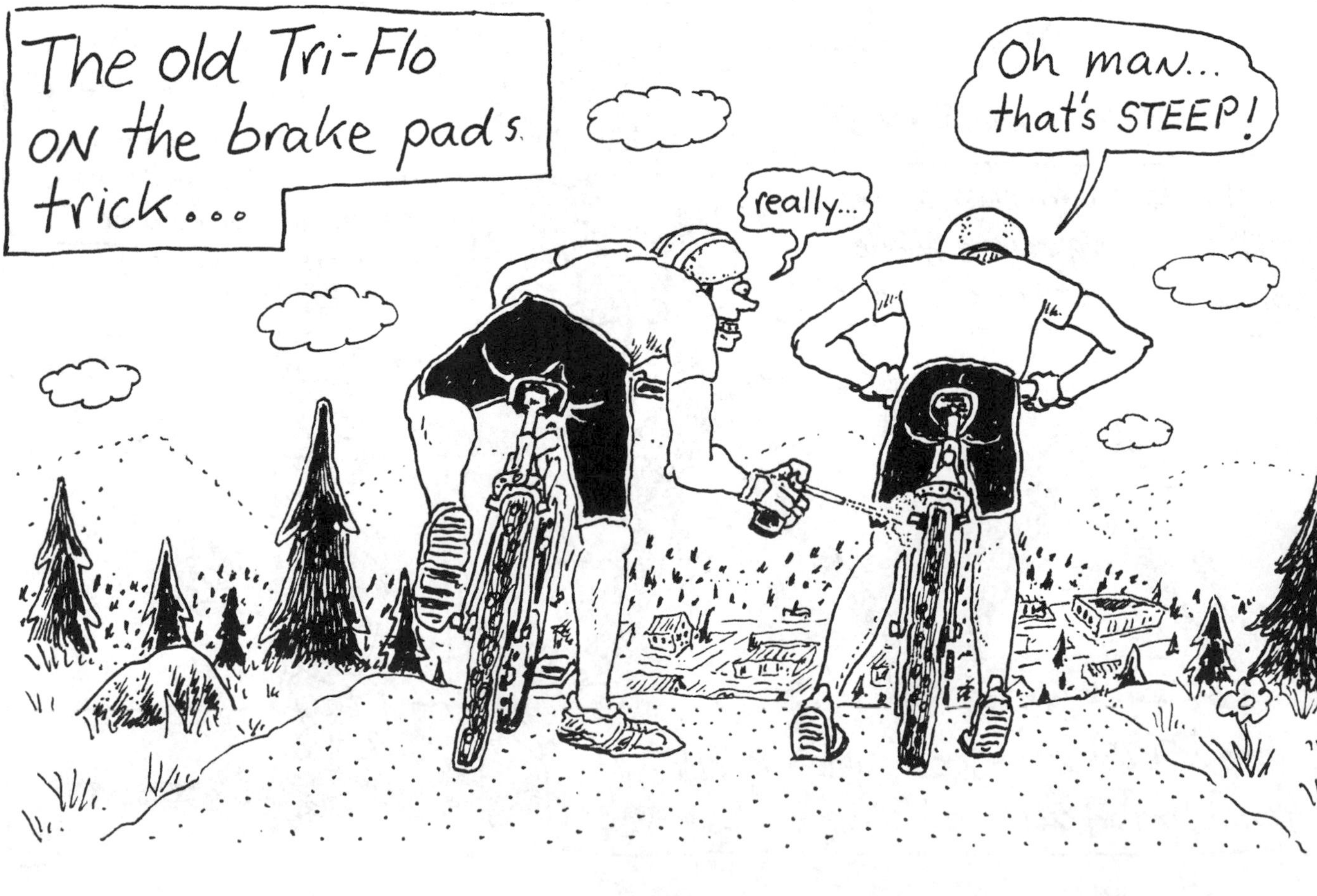
The old Tri-Flo on the brake pads trick...
really...
Oh man... that's STEEP!

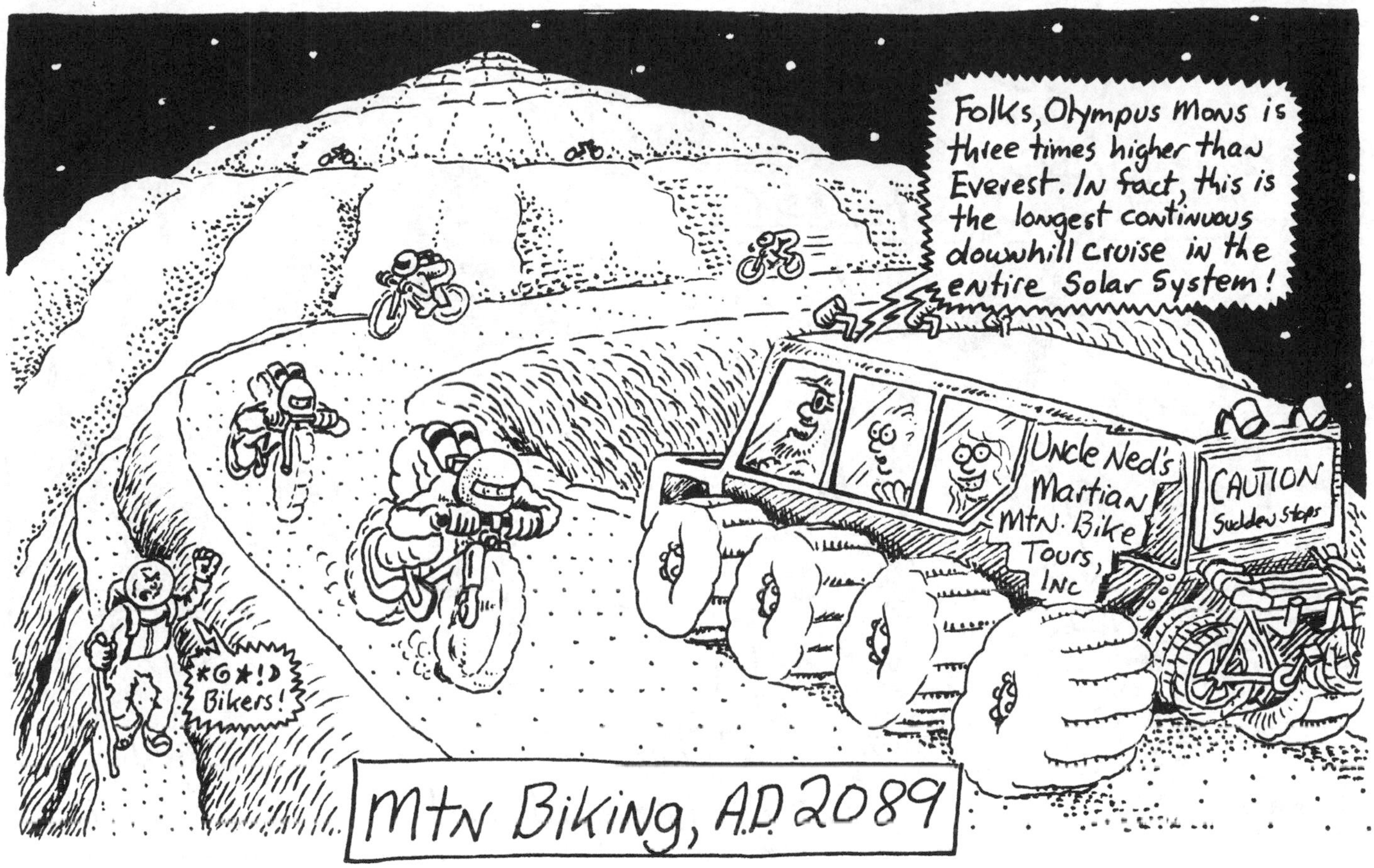
Folks, Olympus Mons is three times higher than Everest. In fact, this is the longest continuous downhill cruise in the entire Solar System!
Uncle Ned's Martian Mtn. Bike Tours, Inc
CAUTION Sudden Stops
*G*!D Bikers!
Mtn Biking, A.D 2089

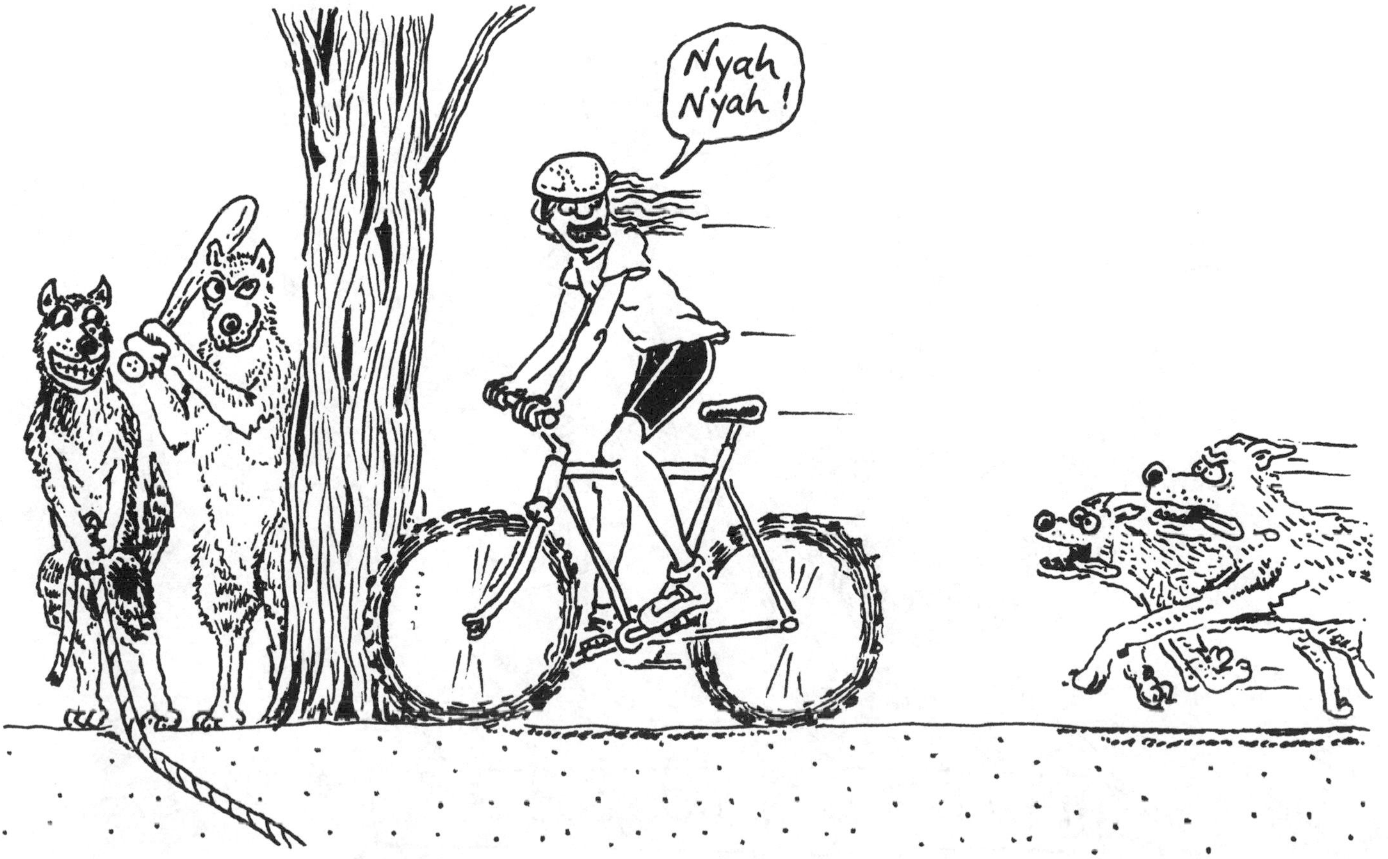
Nyah Nyah!

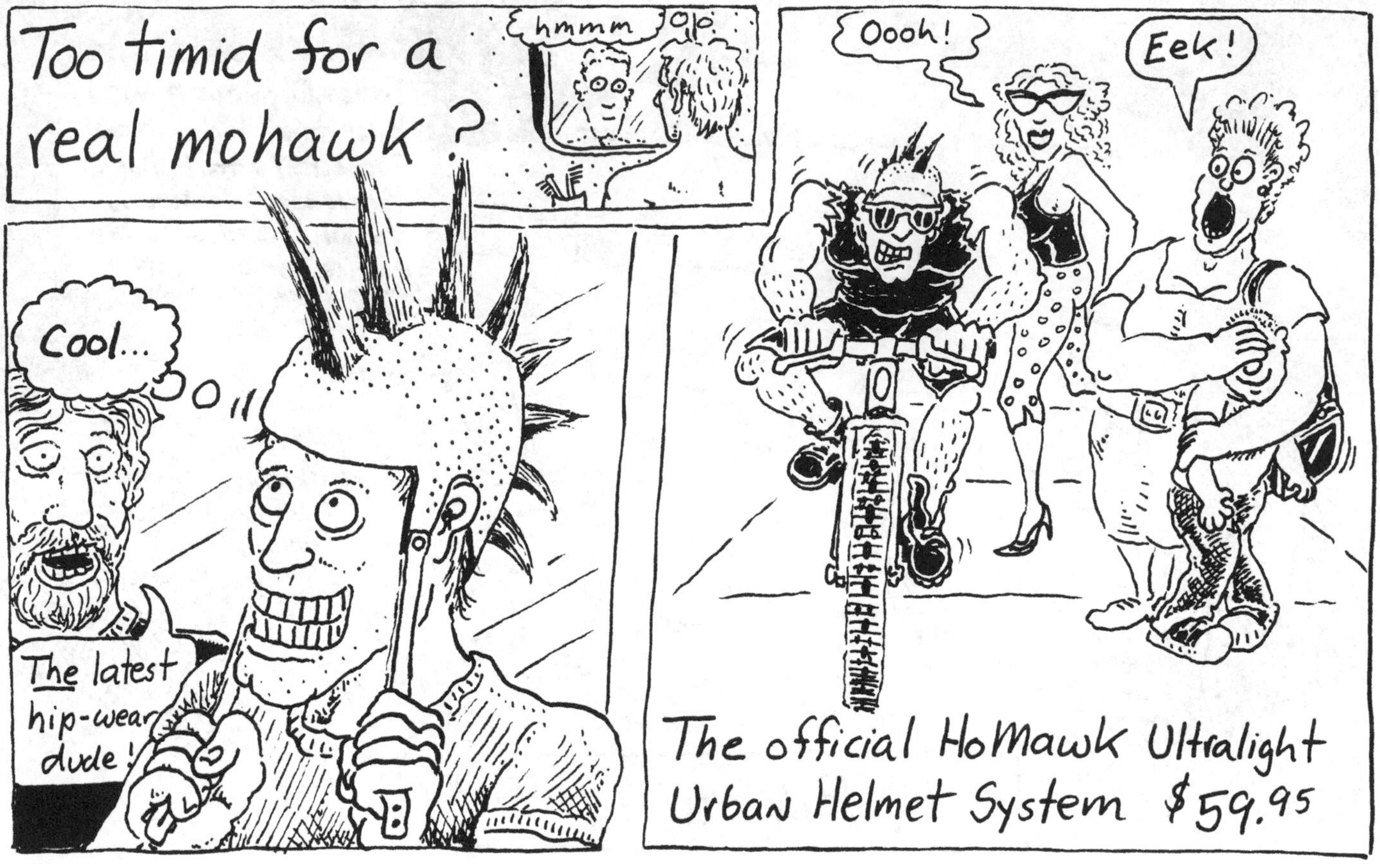
Too timid for a real mohawk?
hmmm
Cool...
The latest hip-wear dude!
Oooh!
Eek!
The official HoMawk Ultralight Urban Helmet System $59.95

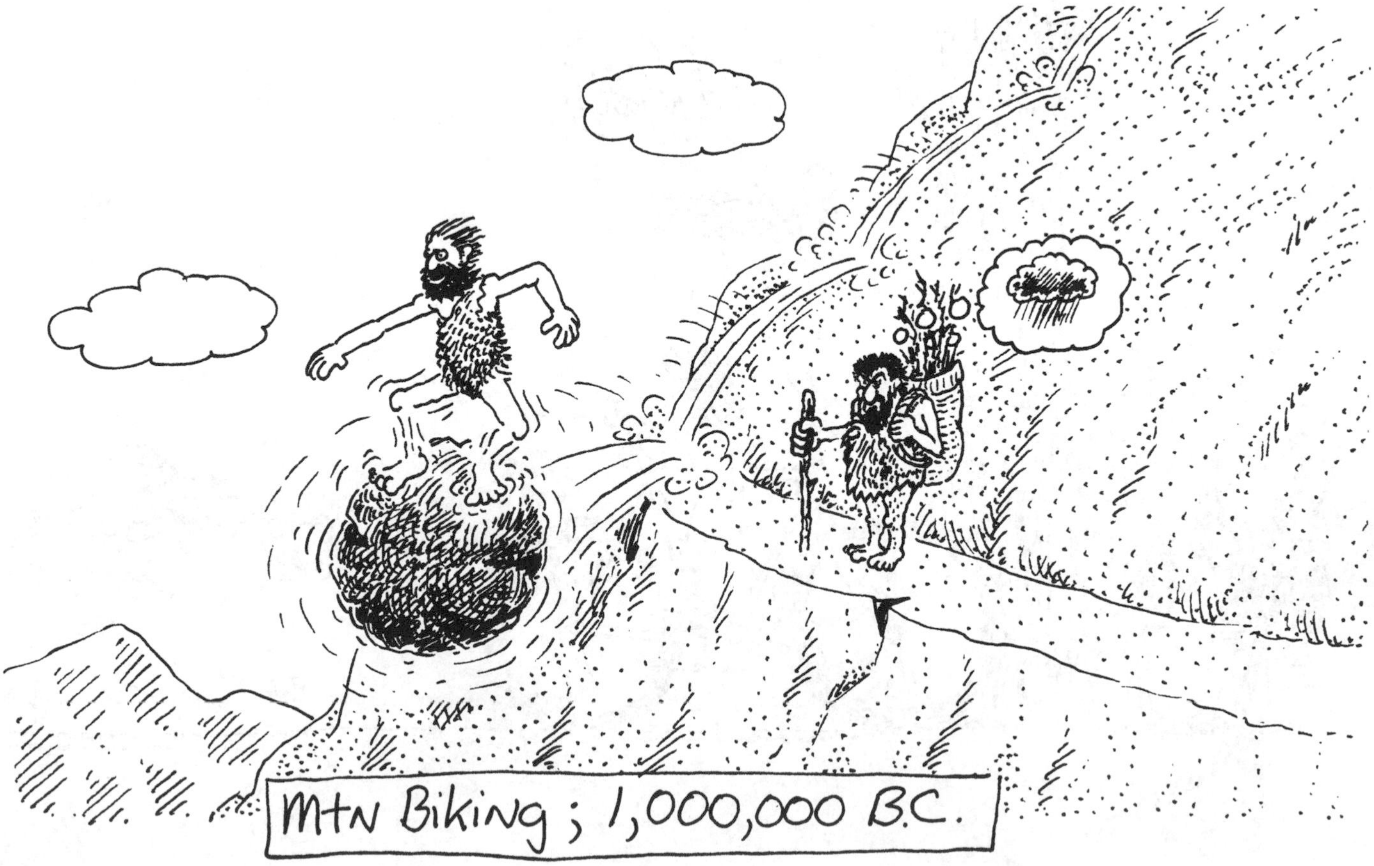
Mtn Biking; 1,000,000 B.C.

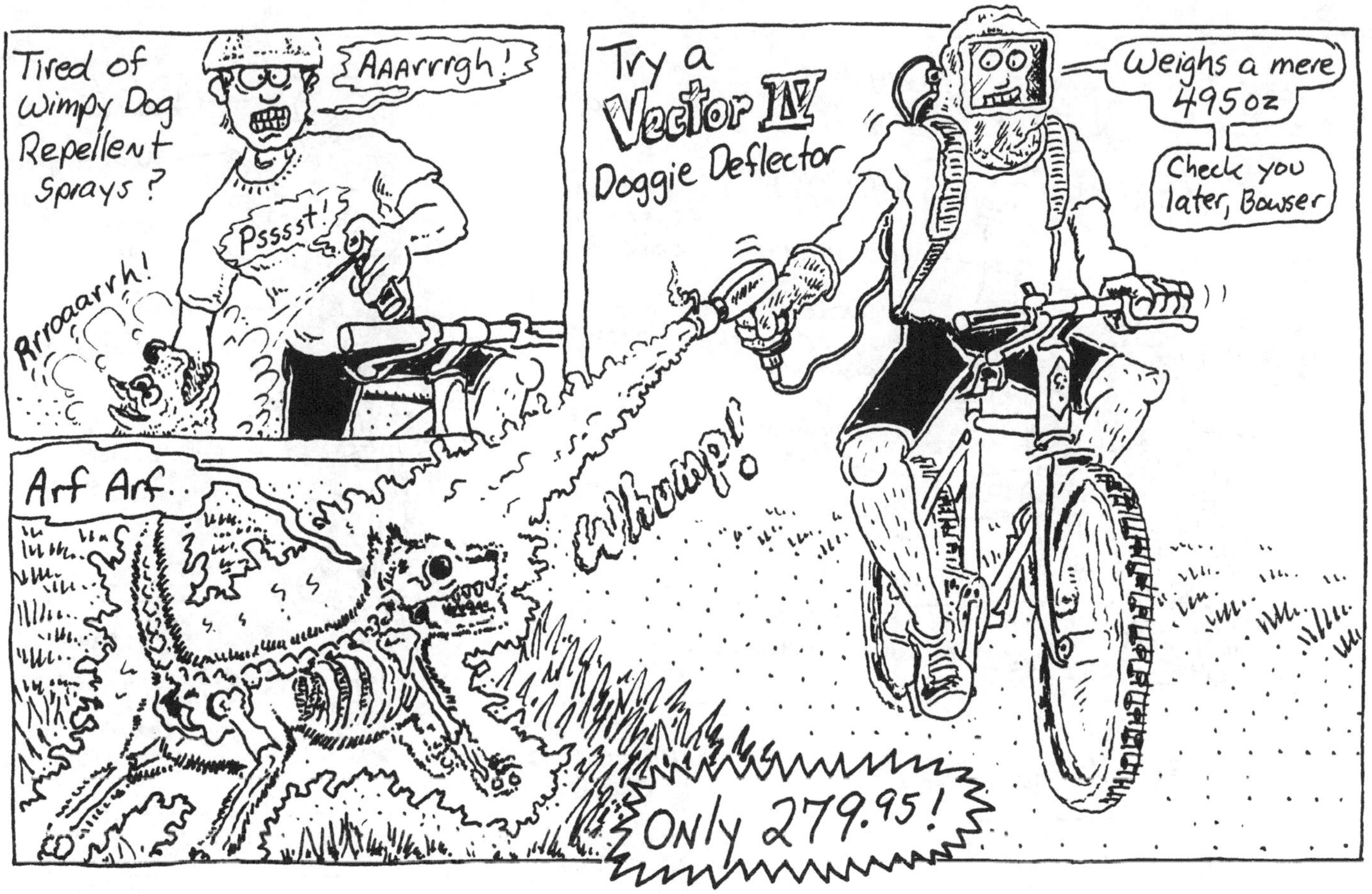
Tired of Wimpy Dog Repellent Sprays?
Aaarrrgh!
Psssst!
Rrroaarrh!
Try a Vector IV Doggie Deflector
Weighs a mere 495 oz
Check you later, Bowser
Arf Arf
Only 279.95!

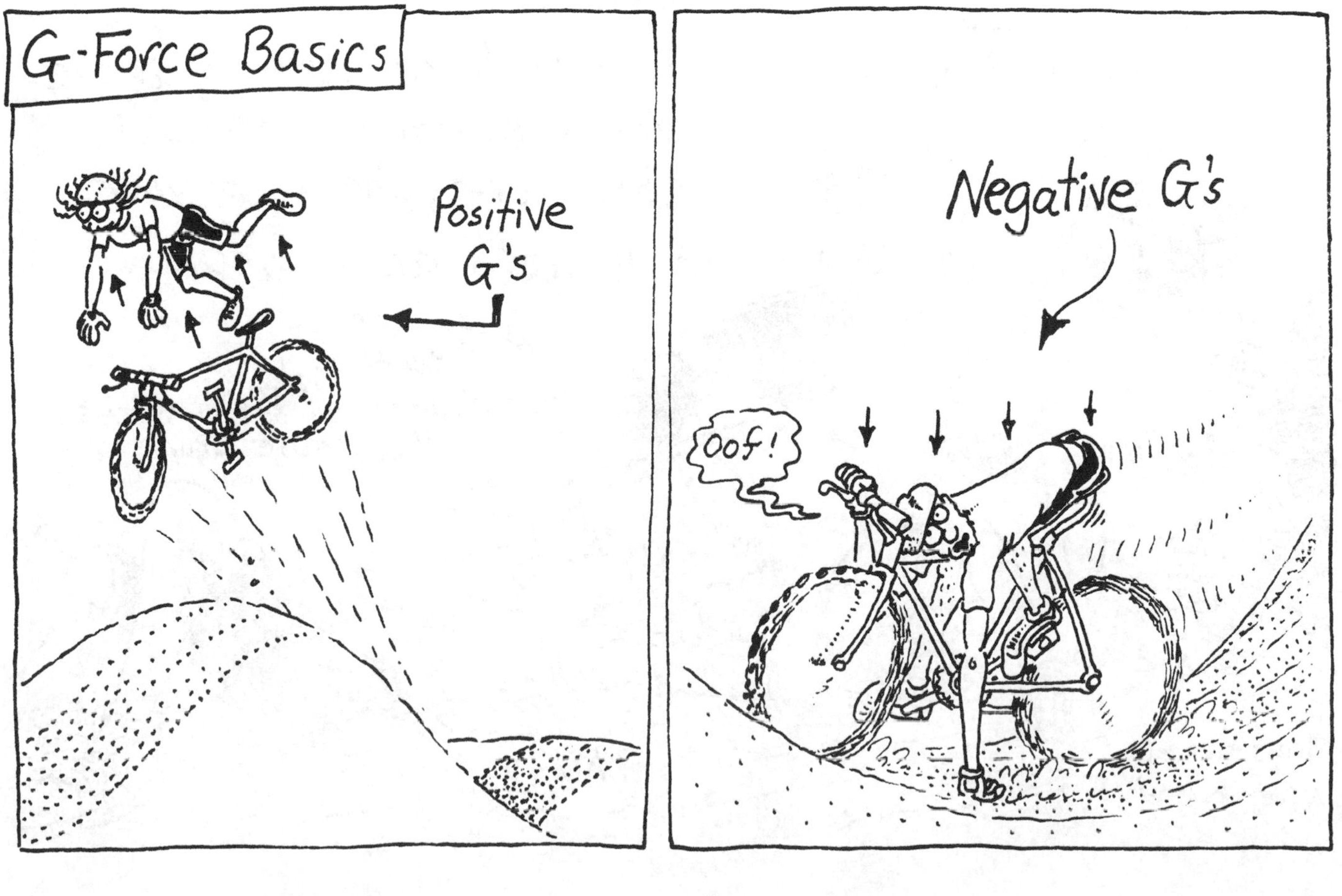
G-Force Basics
Positive G's
Negative G's
Oof!

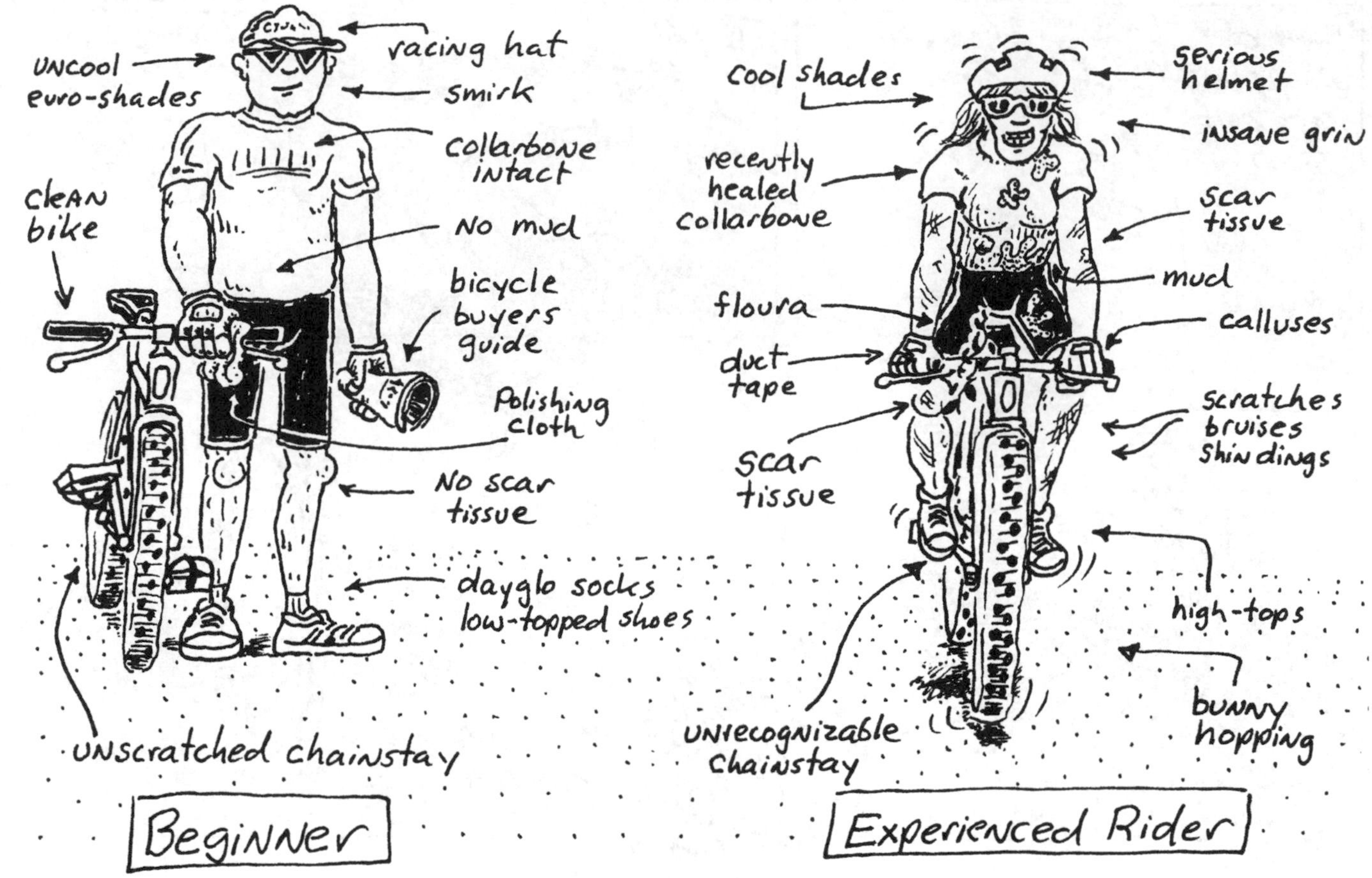
racing hat
uncool euro-shades
smirk
collarbone intact
clean bike
No mud
bicycle buyers guide
Polishing cloth
No scar tissue
dayglo socks low-topped shoes
unscratched chainstay
Beginner
cool shades
serious helmet
insane grin
recently healed collarbone
scar tissue
mud
floura
calluses
duct tape
scratches bruises shin dings
scar tissue
high-tops
bunny hopping
unrecognizable chainstay
Experienced Rider

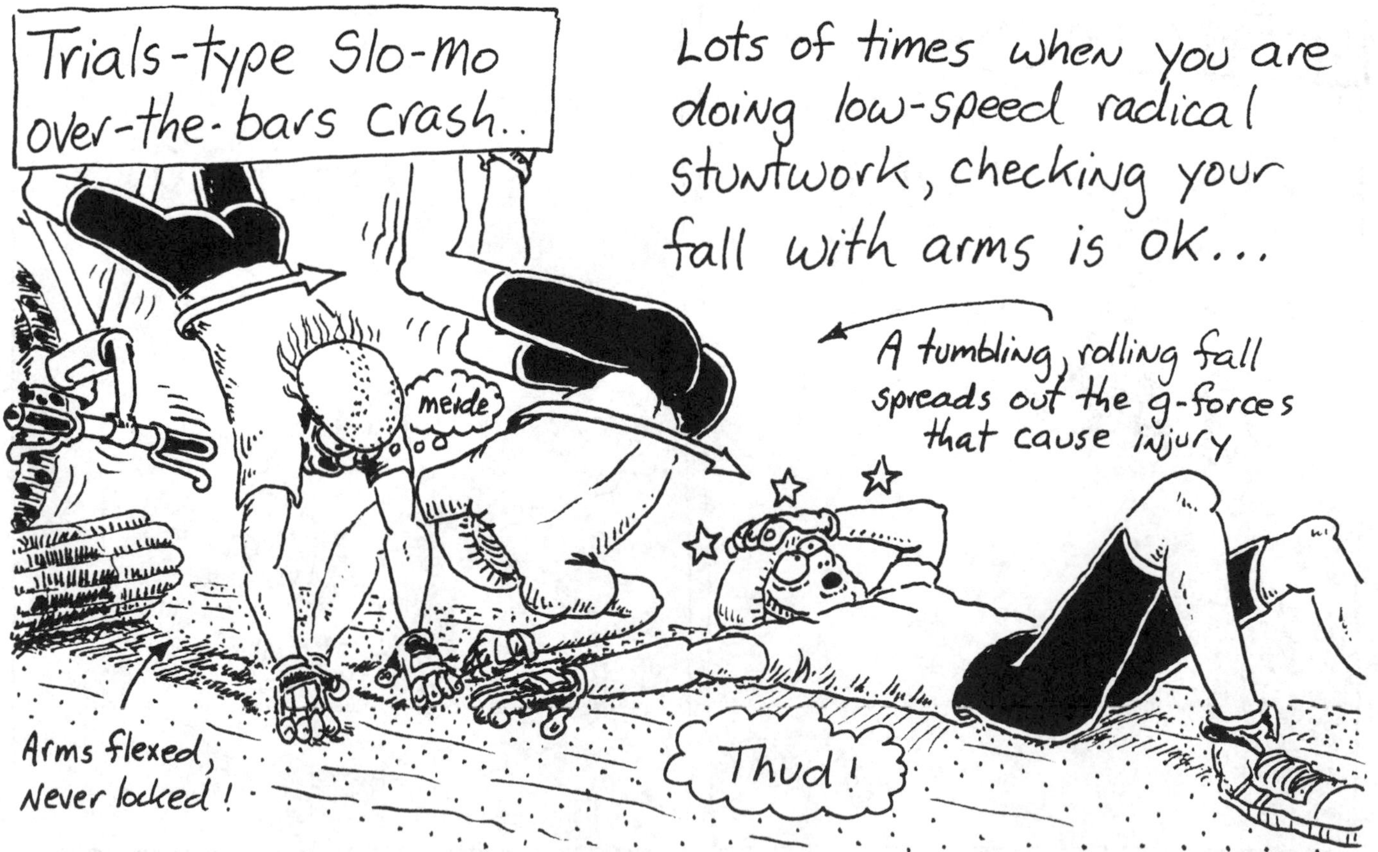
Trials-type Slo-mo over-the-bars crash...
Lots of times when you are doing low-speed radical stuntwork, checking your fall with arms is OK...
merde
A tumbling, rolling fall spreads out the g-forces that cause injury
Arms flexed, Never locked!
Thud!

In a high-speed over-the-bars type crash, staying with the bike greatly lessens your chances of serious injury . . . . . . . . When you go over, arch back, tuck head and think pleasant thoughts . . .

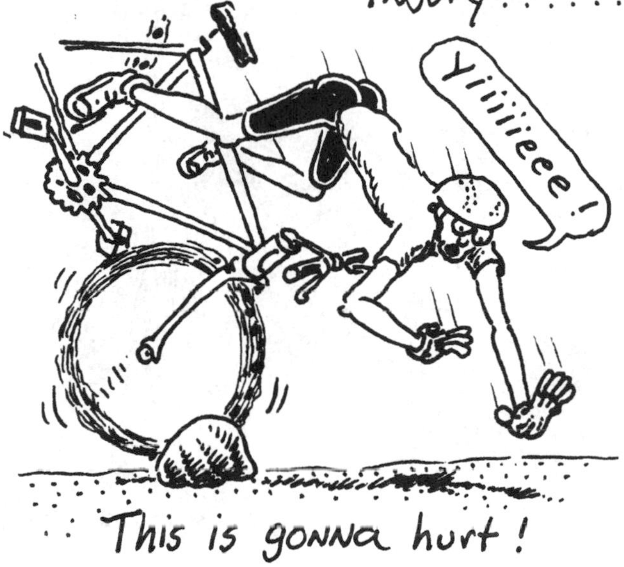
Yiiiiiieee!
This is gonna hurt!

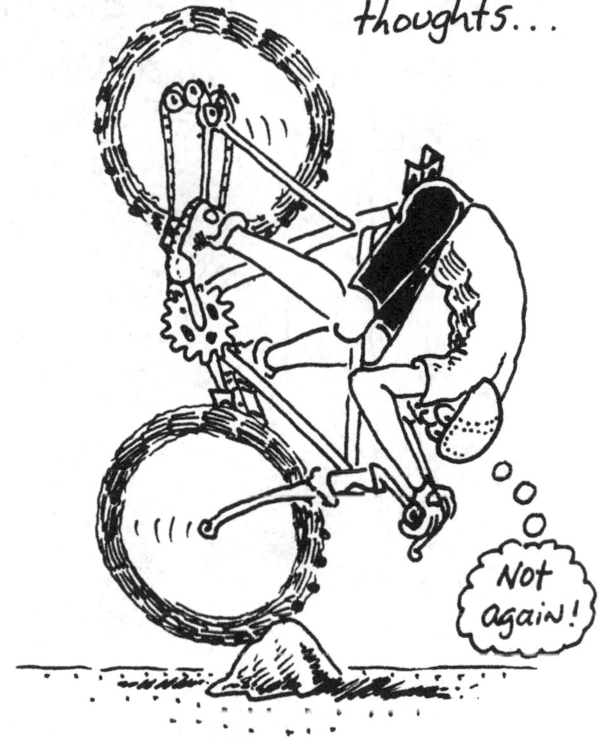
Not again!

If you're real lucky you'll do a complete flip and land on the shoulder area of your back and slide . . .

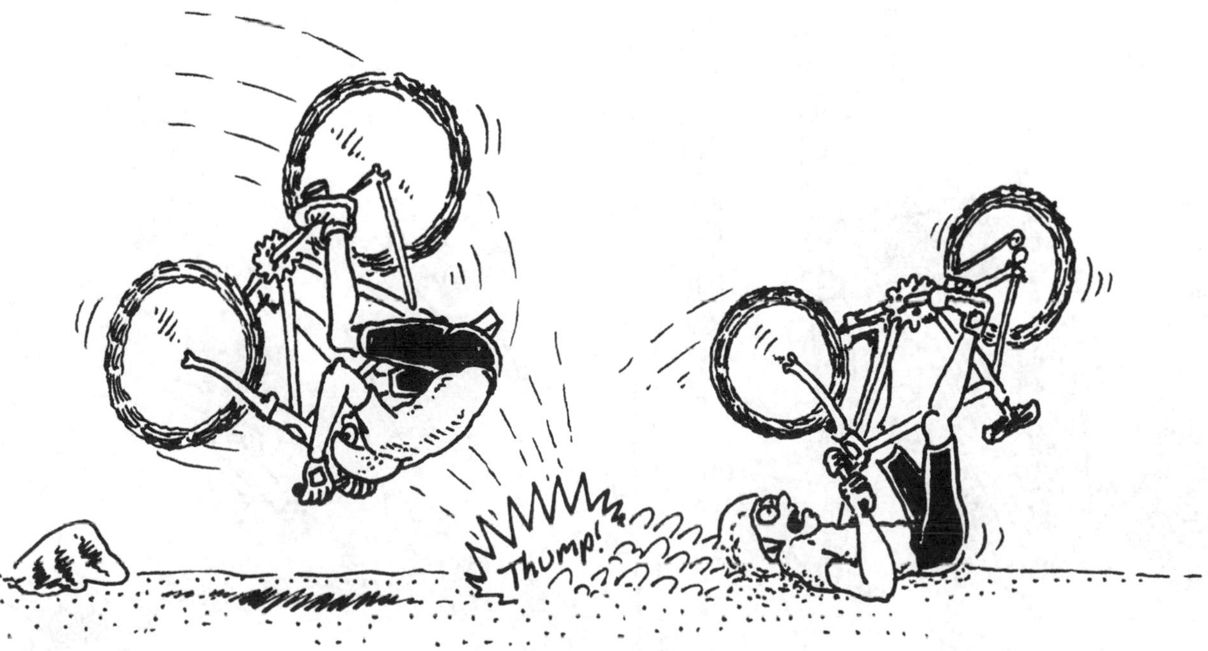
Thump!

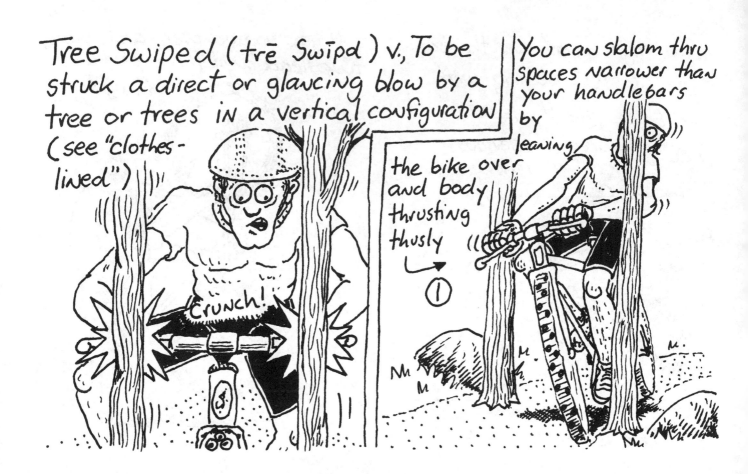

Tree Swiped (trē swīpd) v., To be struck a direct or glancing blow by a tree or trees in a vertical configuration (see "clothes-lined")

You can slalom thru spaces narrower than your handlebars by leaning the bike over and body thrusting thusly ➀

Crunch!

➁

Trees can be contacted intentionally in truly desperate situations...

Clotheslined (clōs·līn·d) v., To be abruptly removed from one's mountain bike by a free-standing horizonal object (tree, cable, etc). See "poled".

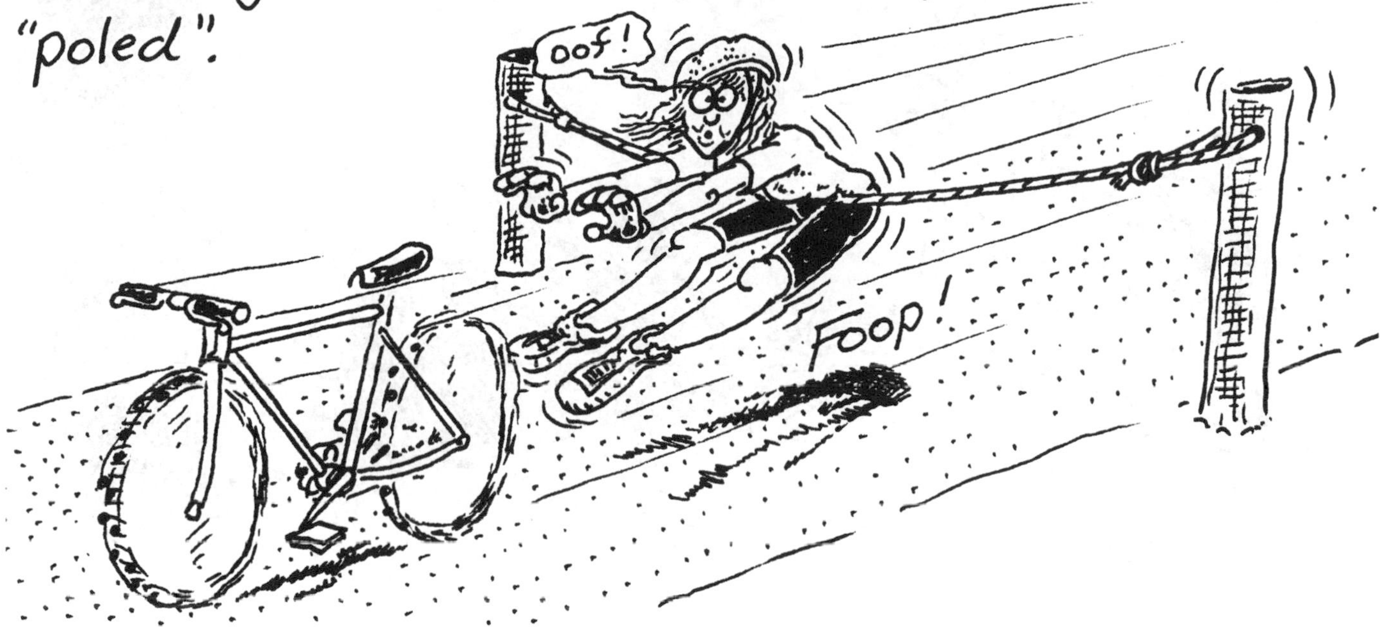
oof!
Foop!

Event Horizon (ə-vēnt hōr-ī-zun) n., Maximum sight distance. As velocity increases, distance to event horizon decreases. (See "First Aid")

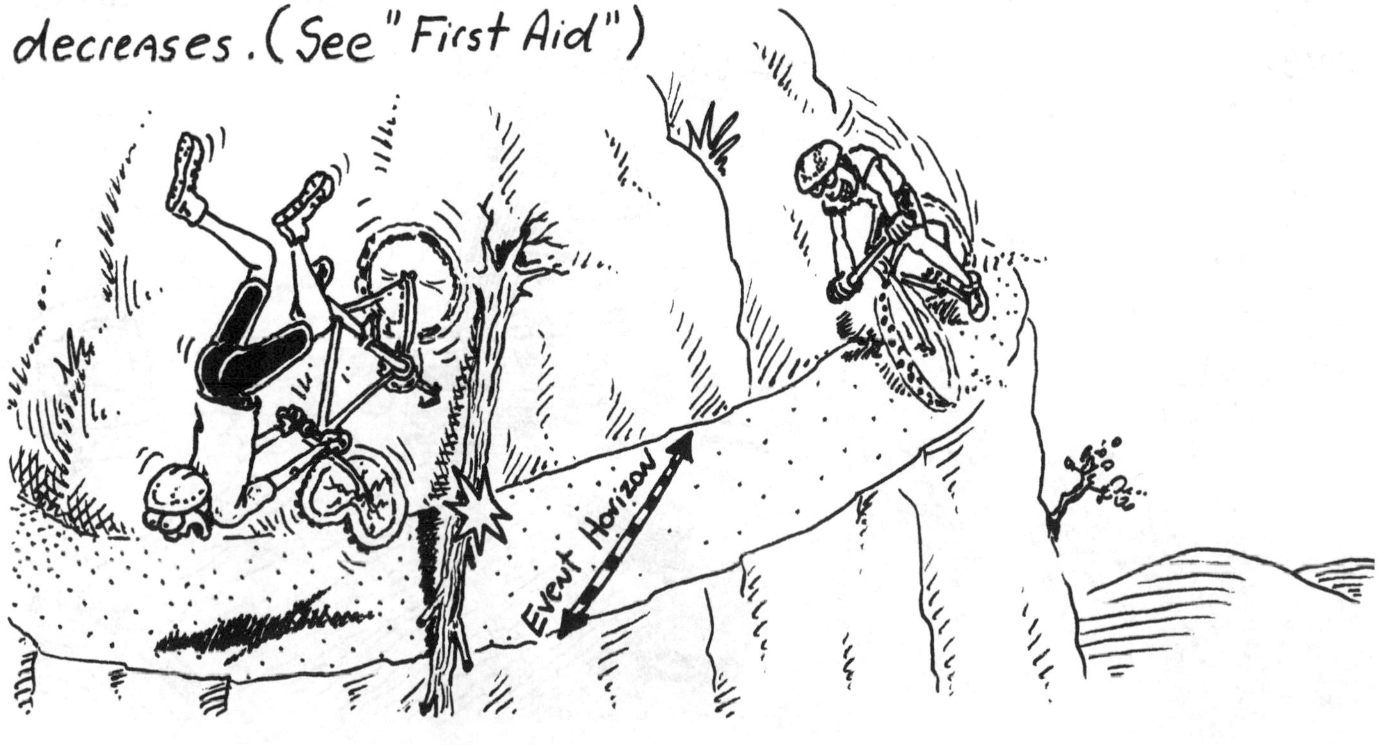
Event Horizon

Mudballing (mūd·bāl·eng) v. To ride in such a way as to become indistinguishable from the terrain...

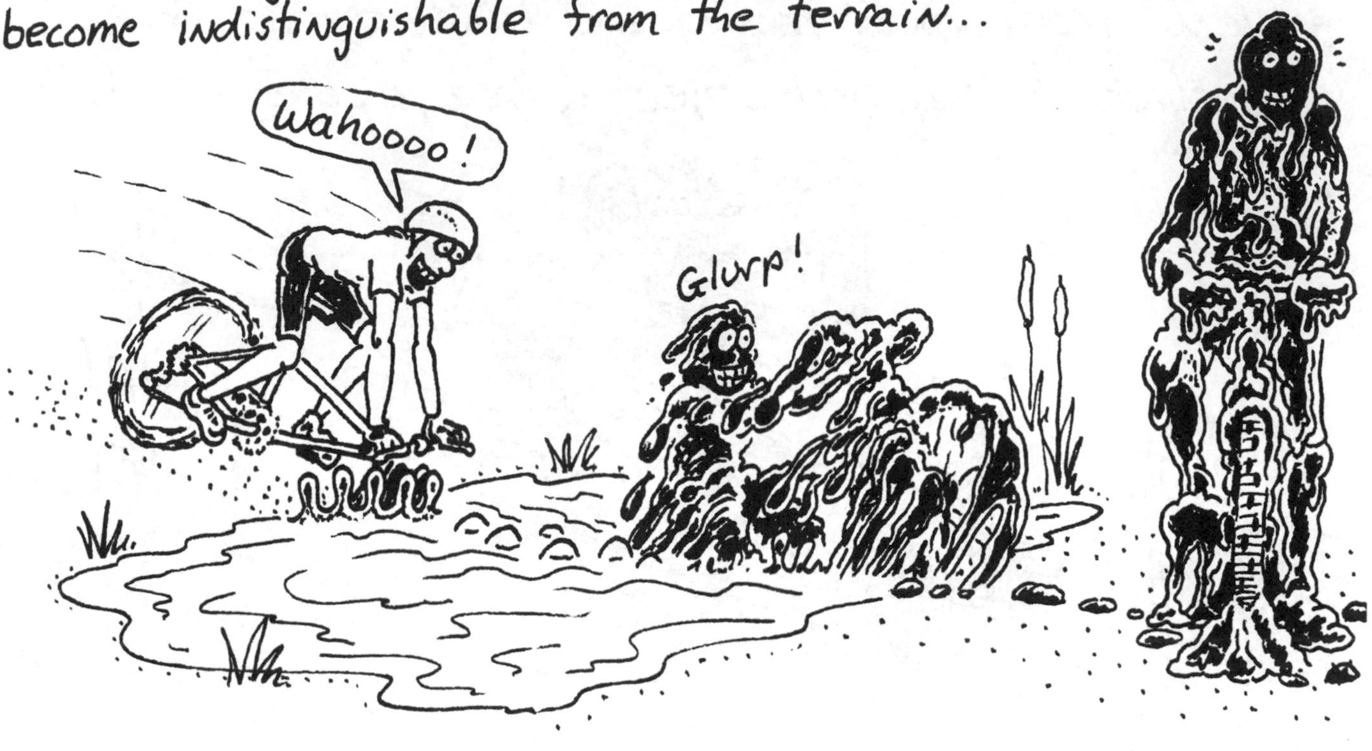
Wahoooo!
Glurp!

Front-pointing (frûnt·poînt·ng) The art of utilizing the outer chainring as a third wheel to climb over logs and other organic obstacles.

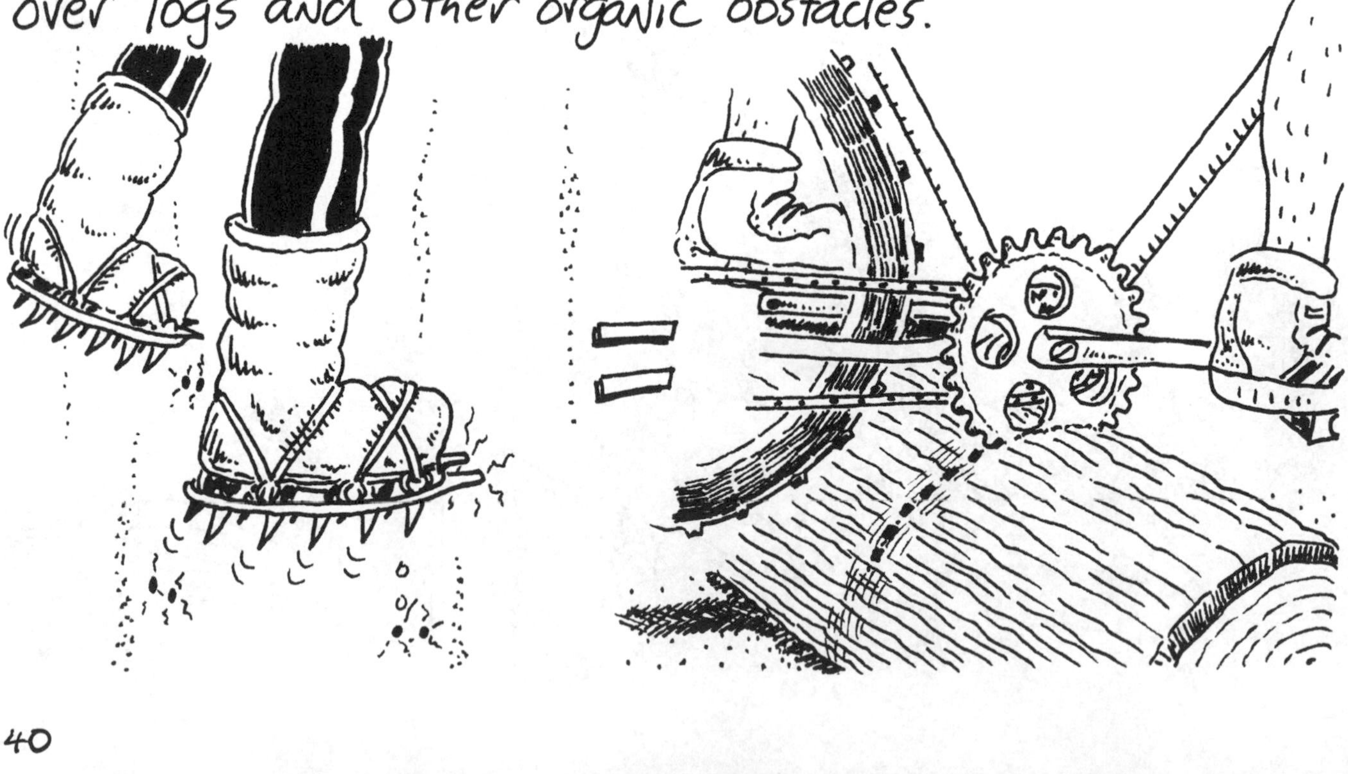

**Fun Hog** (fûn hâwg) n., Any person having a transient "sports-based" lifestyle with obsessive involvement in any or all of the following outdoor sports: rock climbing, river running, mountain biking, alpine skiing, wind surfing, sky diving, fly fishing, etc. Easily recognized by driving ratty-looking utilitarian vehicles festooned with a vast array of equipment worth at least twice the value of the vehicle itself.

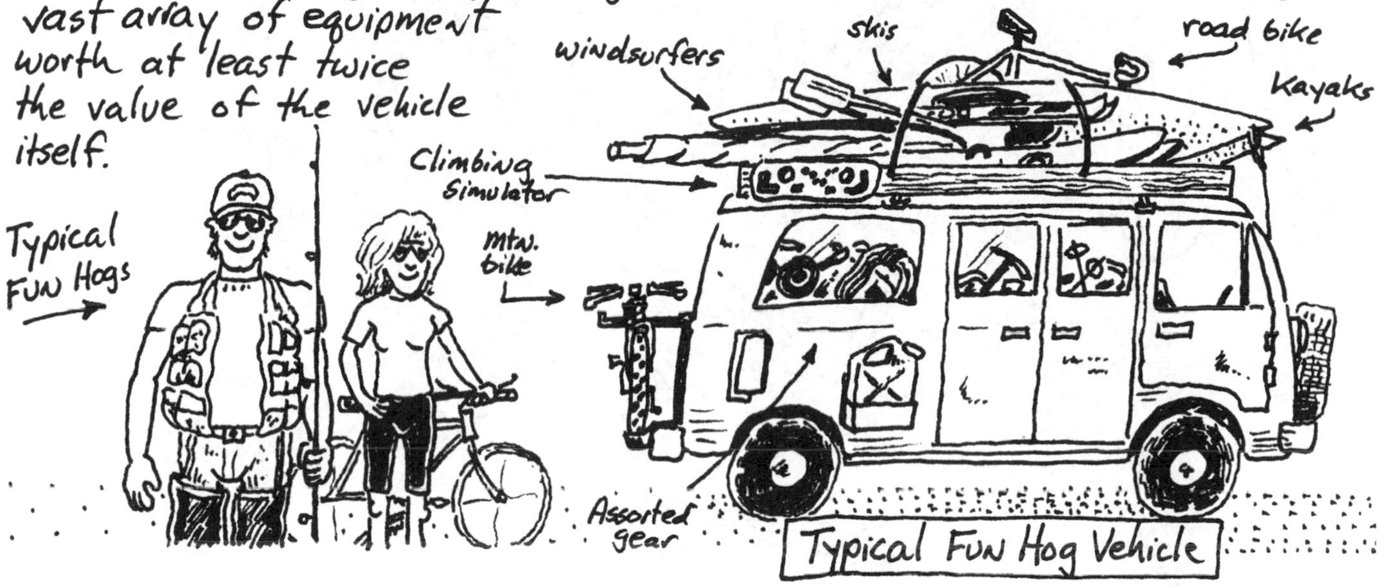
Typical Fun Hogs
mtn. bike
Climbing Simulator
windsurfers
skis
road bike
Kayaks
Assorted gear
Typical Fun Hog Vehicle

**Hell Ride** (a.k.a. "Bataan Death Cruise", "Exploratory Ride", "Humping the Boonies", etc) A pleasure cruise gone wrong due to misdirection, misinformation, or misadventure. Or any combination thereof.

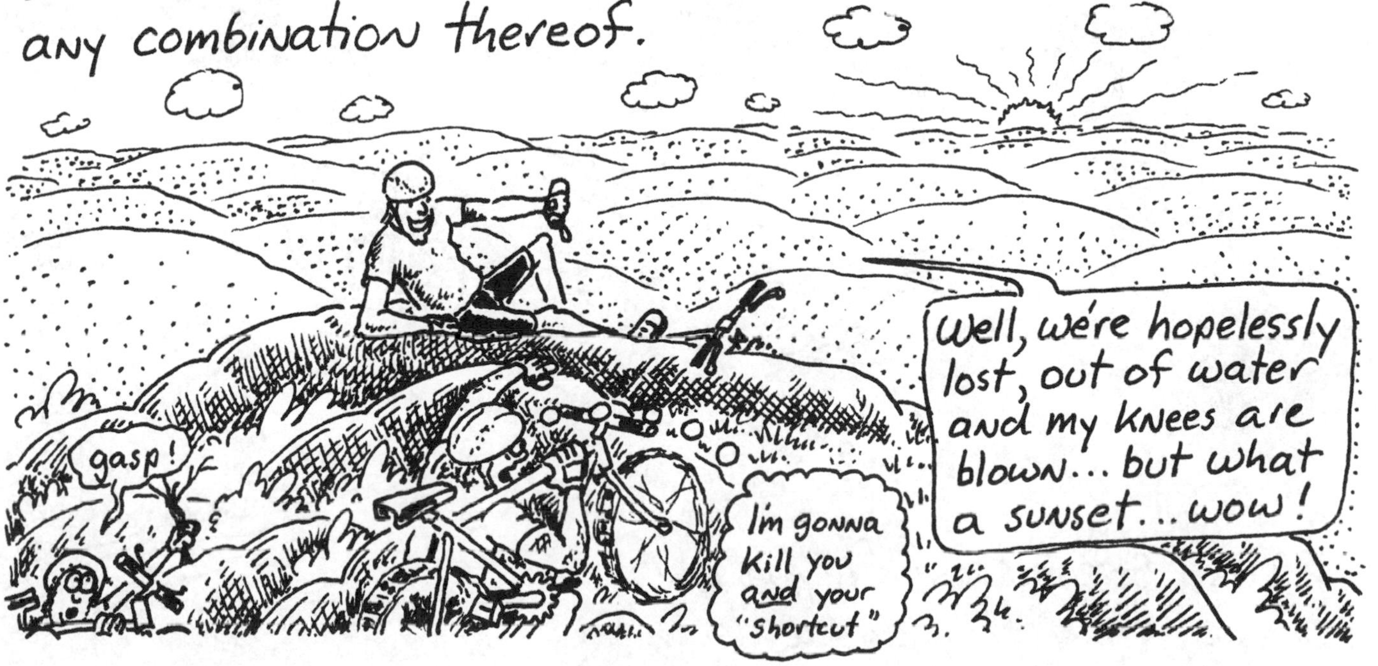
gasp!
Im gonna kill you and your "shortcut"
Well, we're hopelessly lost, out of water and my knees are blown... but what a sunset... wow!

Bear-trapped (bəar tra·pd) v., (a.k.a. "spiked")
To lose one's footing and catch a bear-trap type pedal in the leg, usually the shin...

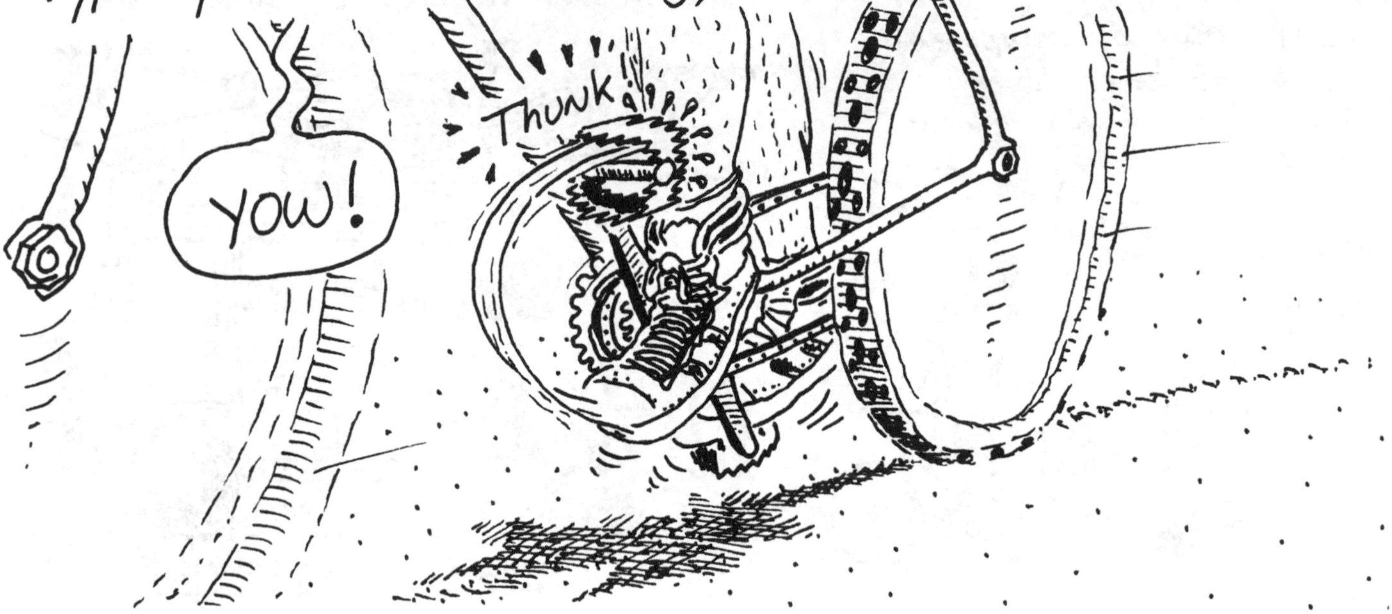
THUNK
YOW!

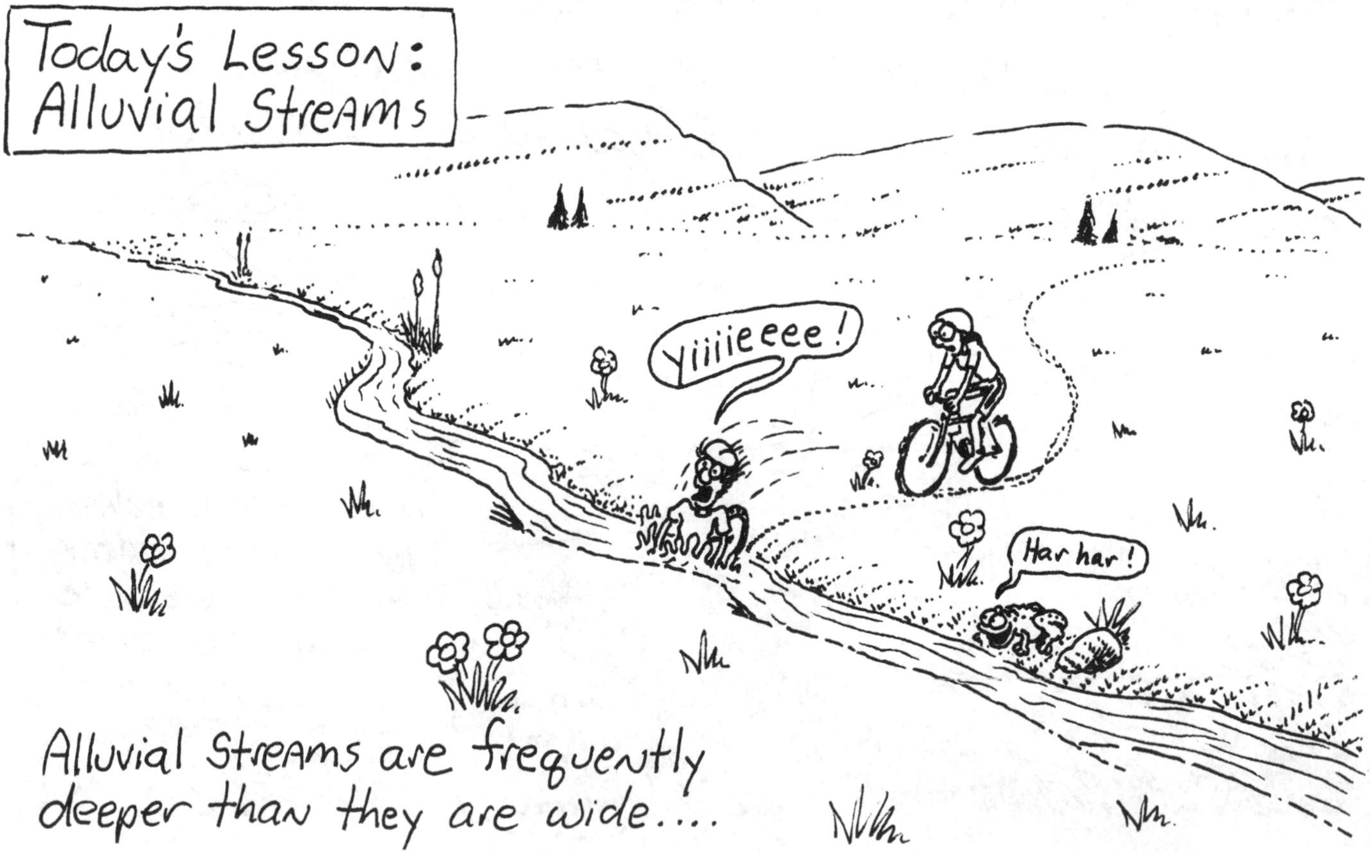
Today's Lesson:
Alluvial Streams
Yiiiieeee!
Har har!
Alluvial streams are frequently deeper than they are wide...

# Dog Evasion Techniques

## Lesson #1 Always be the rider in front!

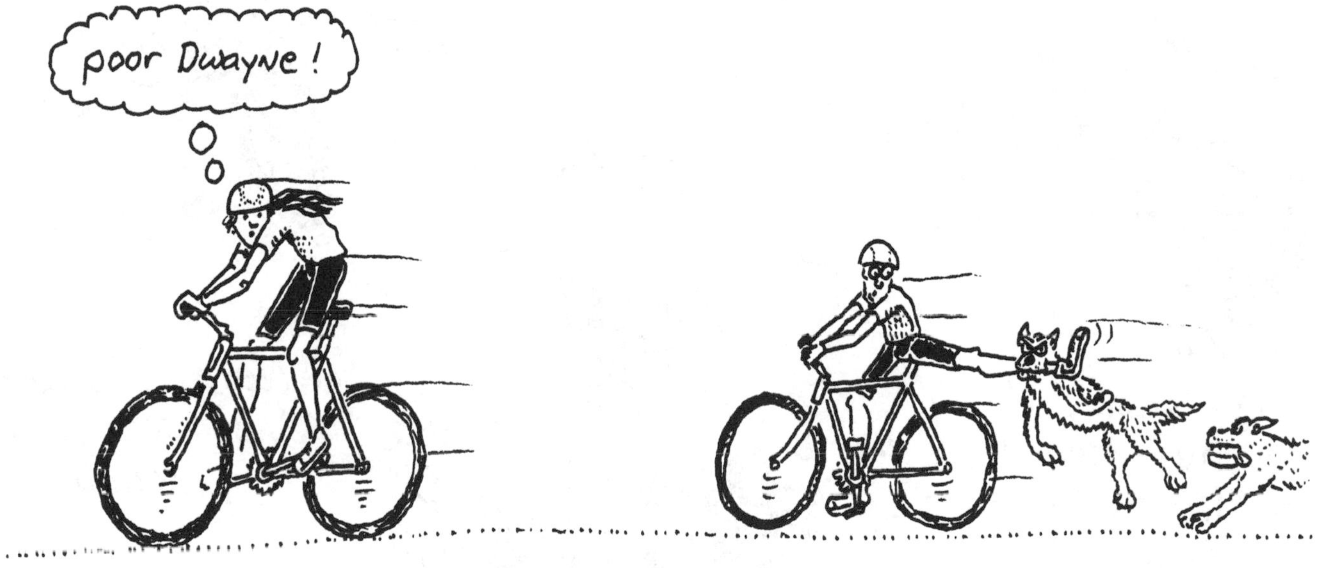

poor Dwayne!


## Advanced Dog Technique

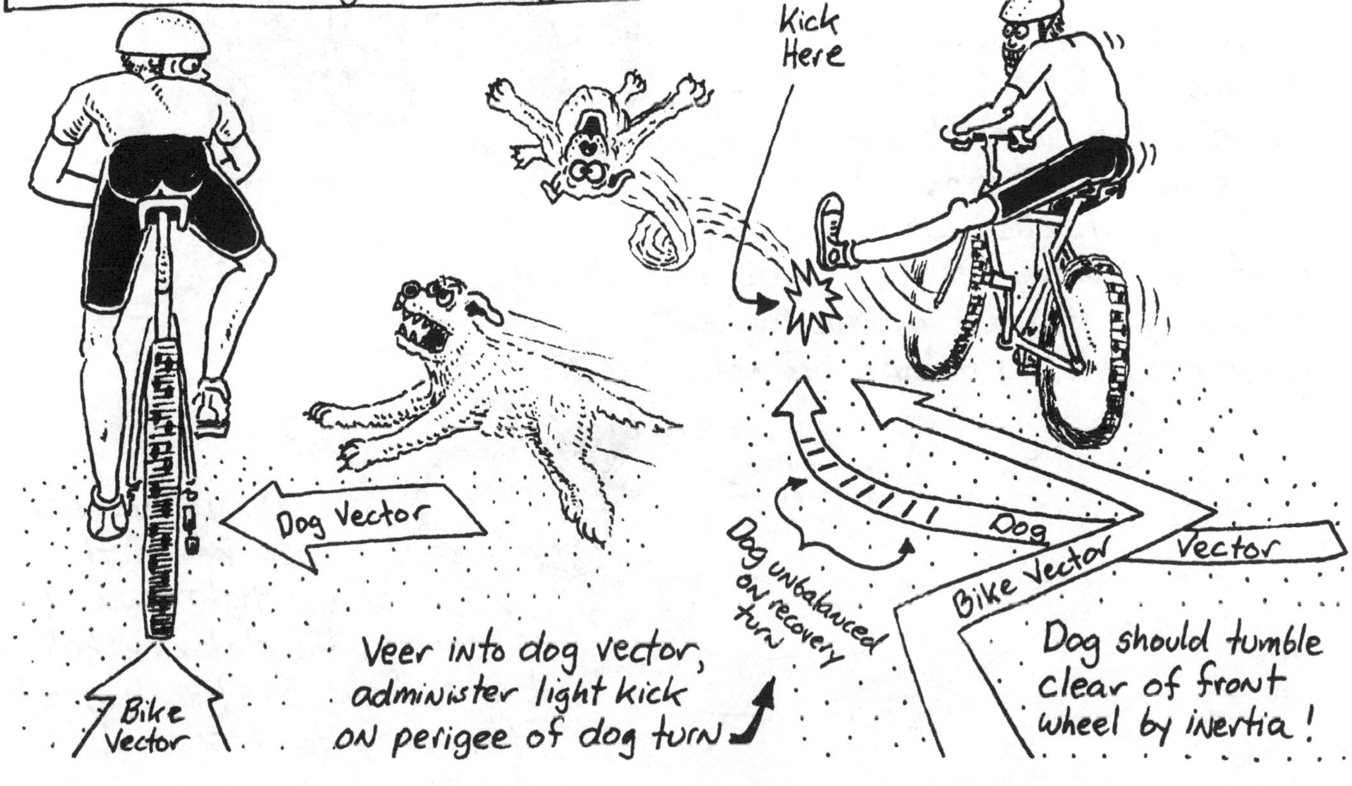

Kick Here
Dog Vector
Dog Vector
Bike Vector
Dog unbalanced on recovery turn
Bike Vector
Veer into dog vector, administer light kick on perigee of dog turn
Dog should tumble clear of front wheel by inertia!

# The Great Brake Debate

Or "How many fingers per brake lever under what conditions?"

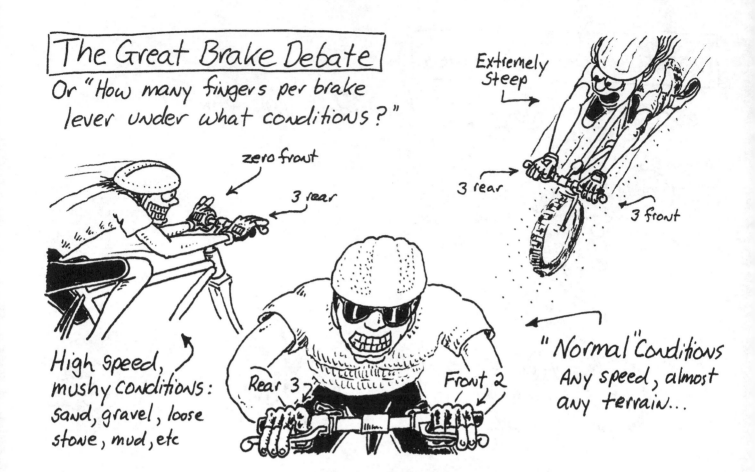

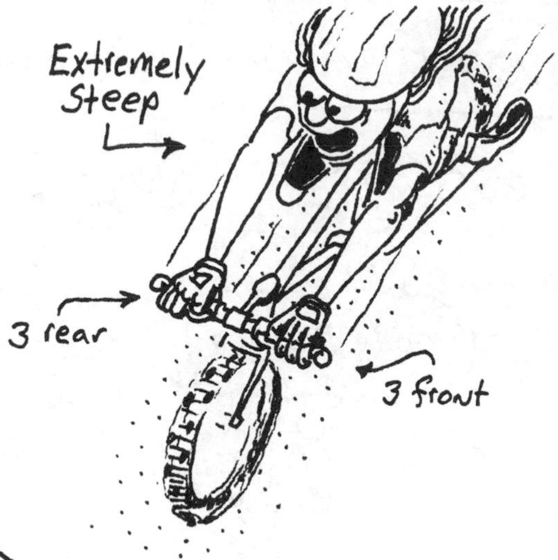
Extremely Steep
3 rear
3 front

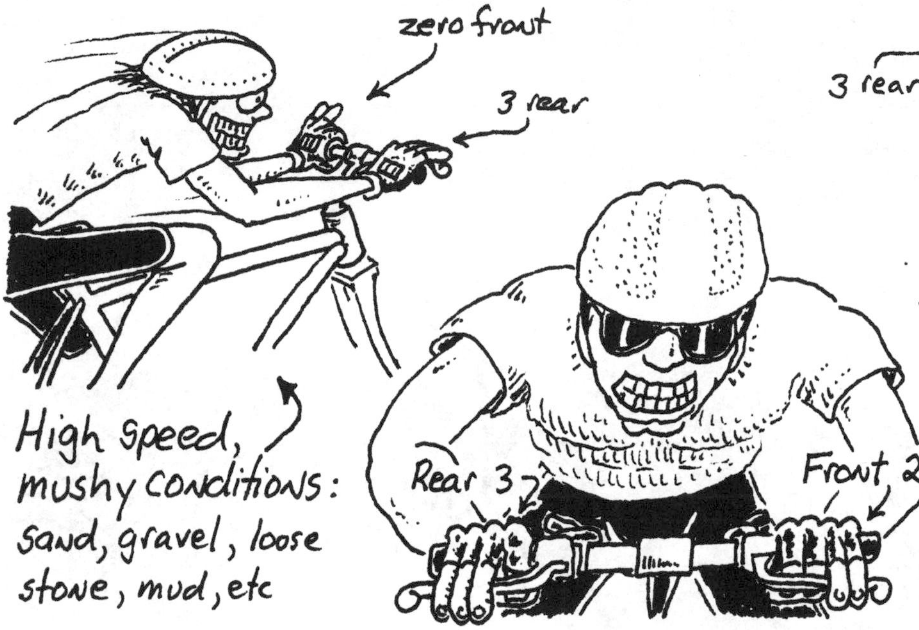
zero front
3 rear
Rear 3
Front 2

High speed, mushy conditions: sand, gravel, loose stone, mud, etc

"Normal" Conditions
Any speed, almost any terrain...

# All about "Chain Suck"

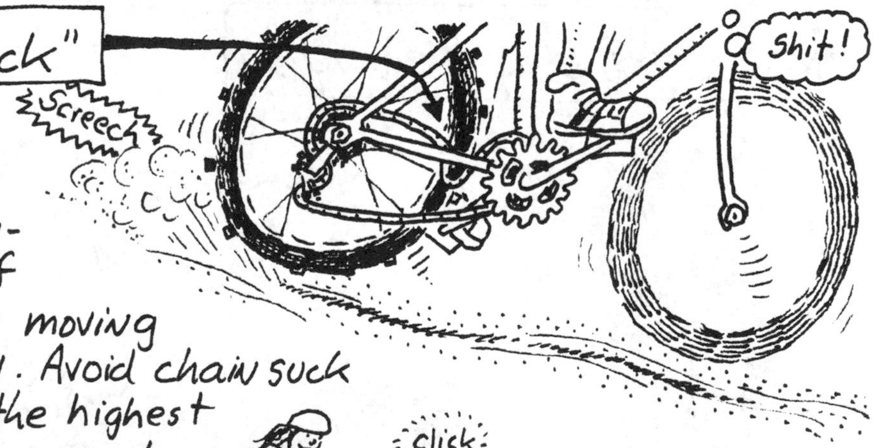
Screech
Shit!

Chain suck is usually the result of bad technique... the rider downshifts in anticipation of a steep obstacle while moving fast on bumpy terrain. Avoid chain suck by always staying in the highest gear possible on bumpy ground...

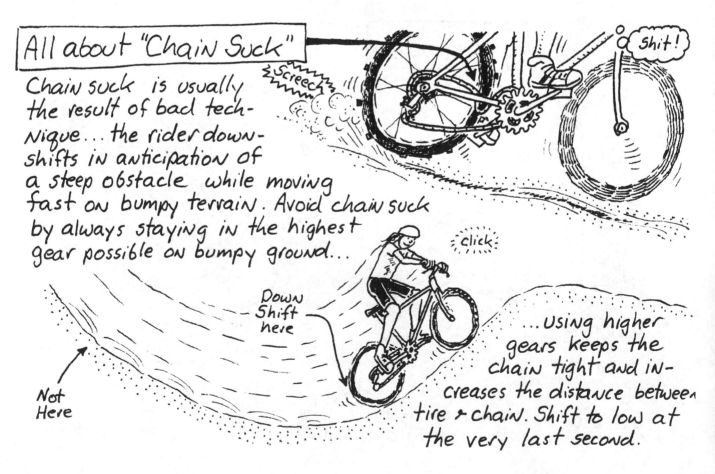

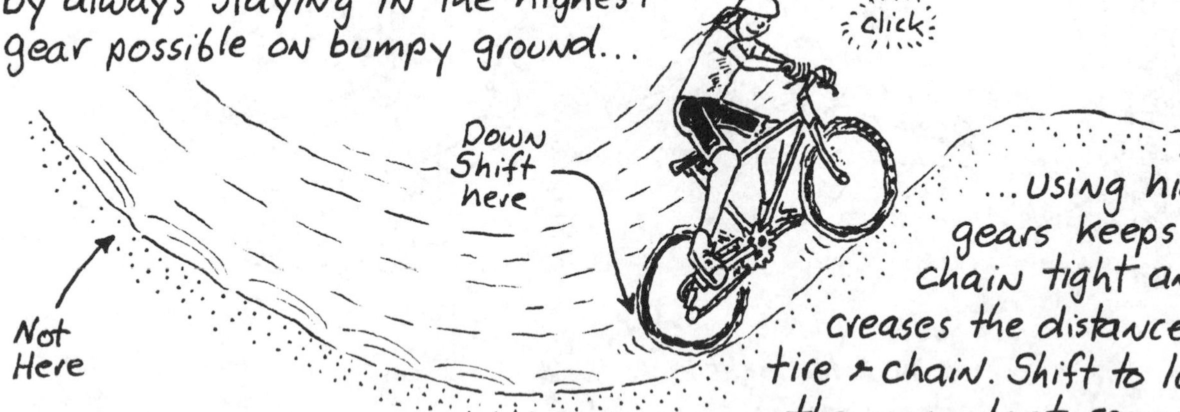
click
Down Shift here
Not Here

...using higher gears keeps the chain tight and increases the distance between tire & chain. Shift to low at the very last second.

# Horse Etiquitte

Mountain bikes are the new critters in the woods. Over time, horses will get habituated to us but right now we are frightening to most of them. In a horse/Mtn. Bike encounter always dismount and give the horse the right of way...

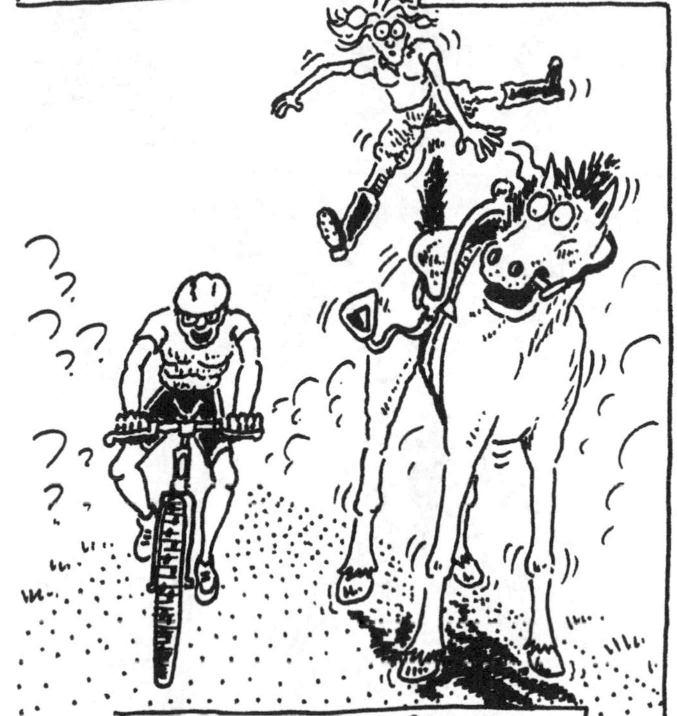

Please Refrain from this!

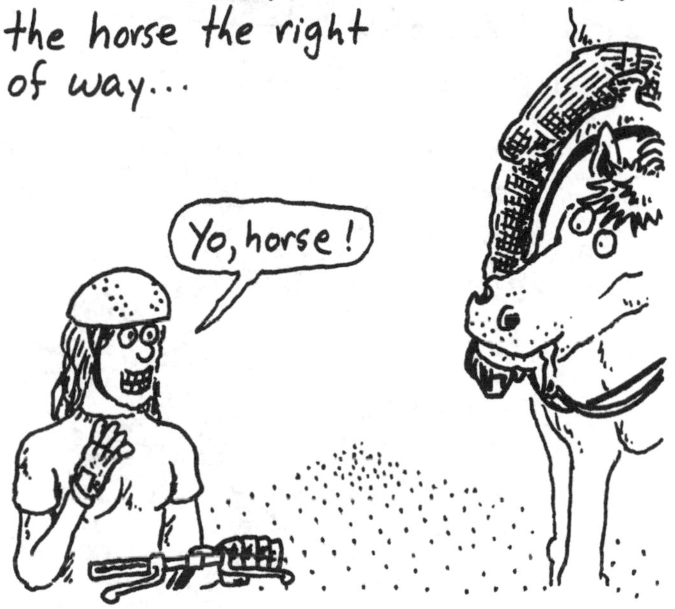
Yo, horse!

Dismount and stand on the downhill side of trail. Stay in horse's line of vision, talk reassuringly. Remount only when horse is at least 100 feet away...

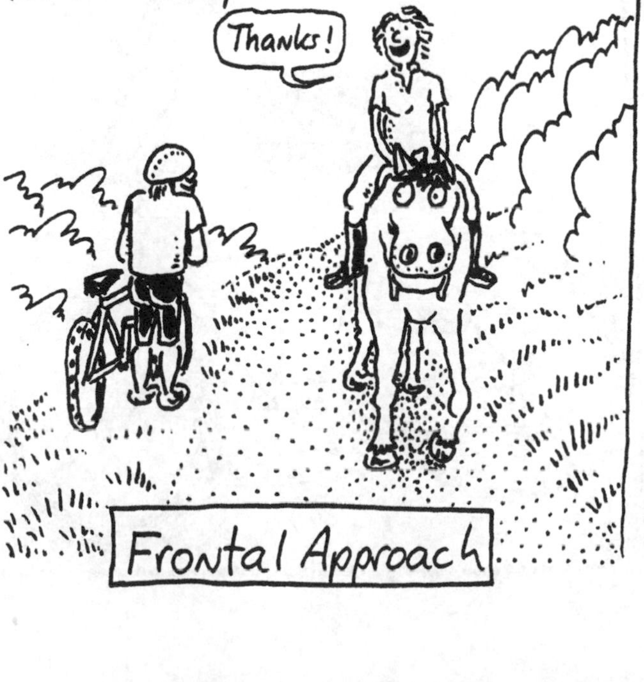
Thanks!

Frontal Approach

Hang well back until horseperson notices you. Usually they will move off the trail to allow you to walk your bike past. Remount at minimum 100' past horse.

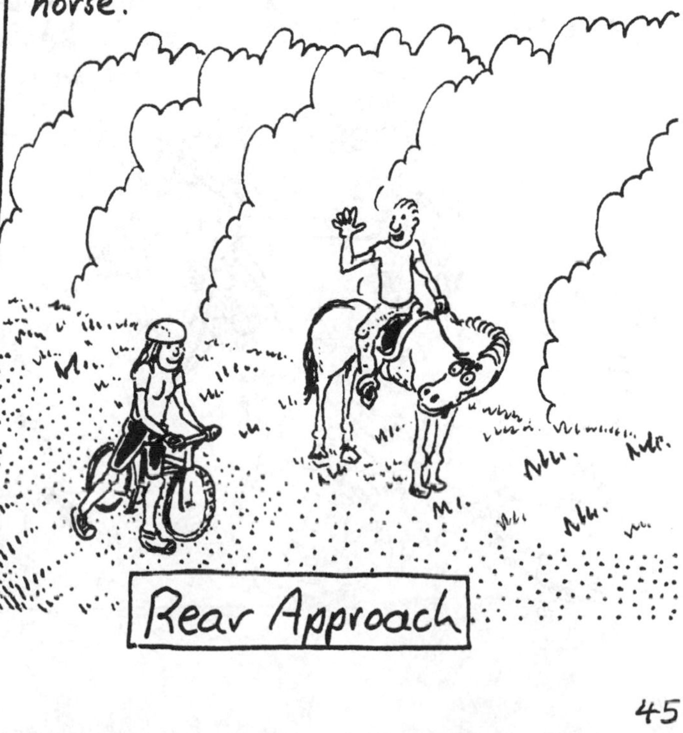

Rear Approach

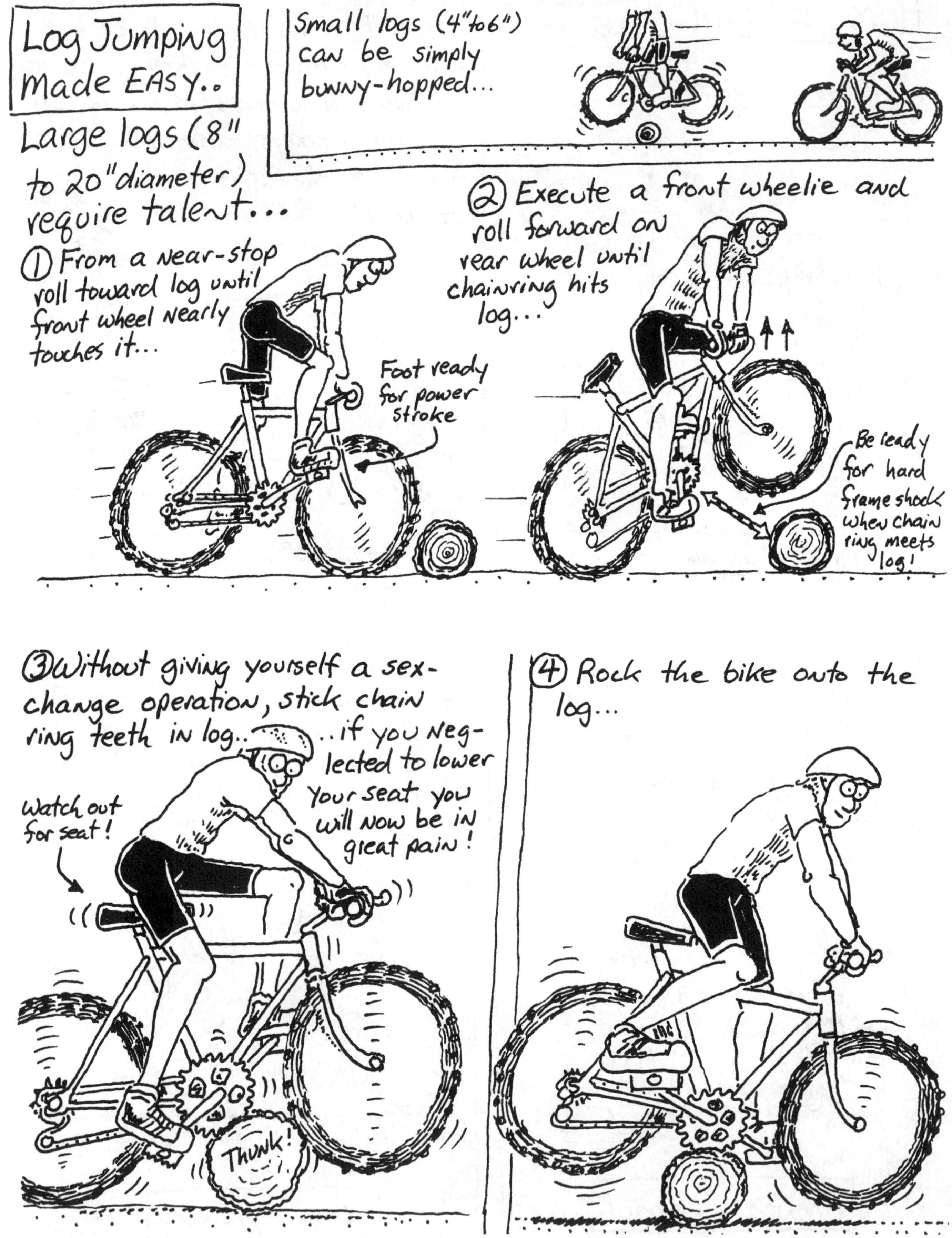

Log Jumping Made EASY..
Small logs (4" to 6") can be simply bunny-hopped...
Large logs (8" to 20" diameter) require talent...
① From a near-stop roll toward log until front wheel nearly touches it...
Foot ready for power stroke
② Execute a front wheelie and roll forward on rear wheel until chainring hits log...
Be ready for hard frame shock when chain ring meets log!
③ Without giving yourself a sex-change operation, stick chain ring teeth in log...
..if you neglected to lower your seat you will now be in great pain!
Watch out for seat!
THUNK!
④ Rock the bike onto the log...

⑤ Pedal over log on chain ring and rock front wheel onto ground...

⑥ Throw weight over front wheel to bring rear wheel over log..

Toe nudge if necessary

⑦ Finish standing with knees flexed...

Caution: if you hit the log too hard with your chain ring (Step #3) you get a seat in the naughty parts. Always go slow & lower seat to jump logs

Watch that seat!

Thump

OOOF!

THUNK!

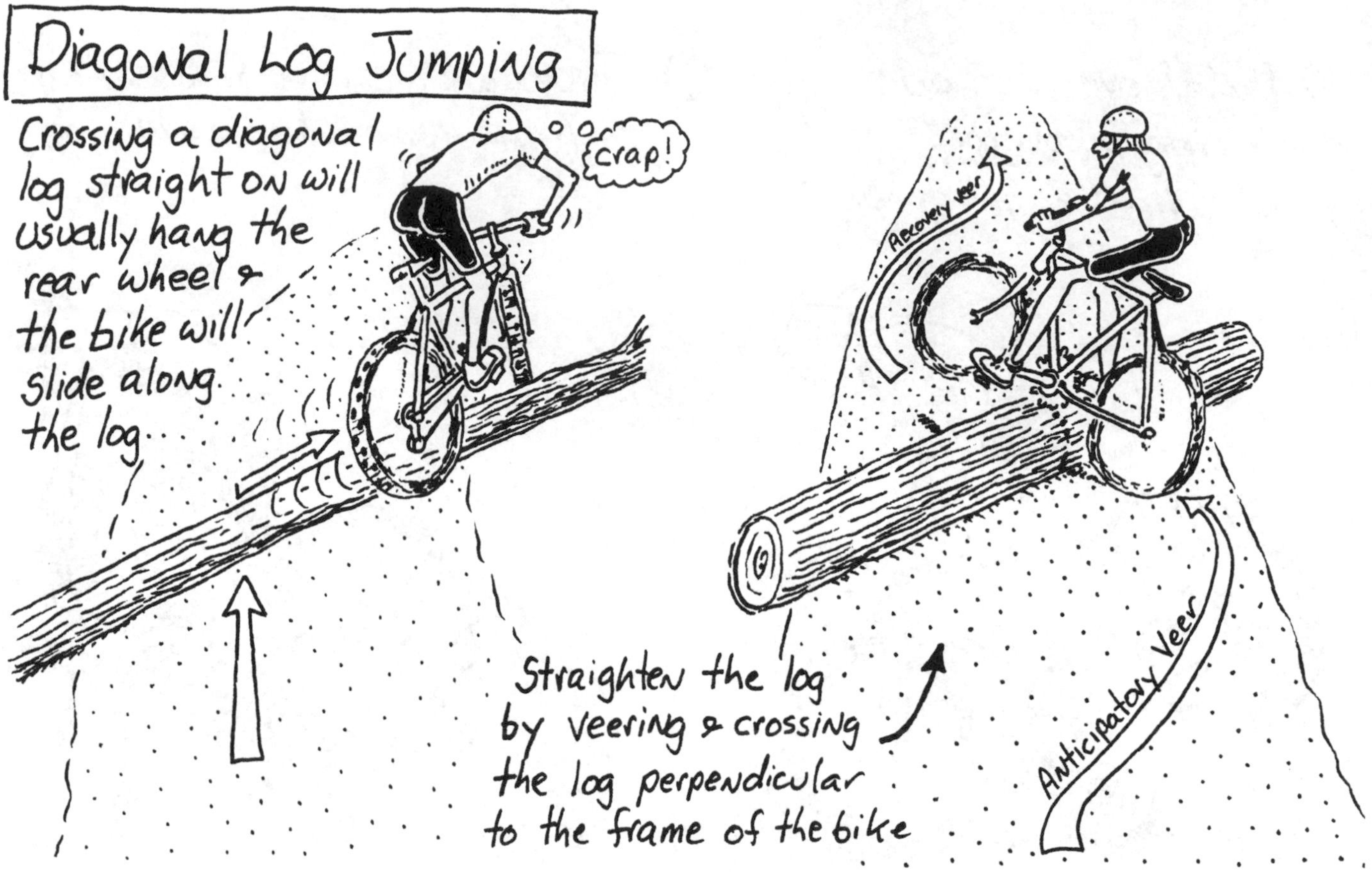
Diagonal Log Jumping
Crossing a diagonal log straight on will usually hang the rear wheel & the bike will slide along the log.
crap!
Recovery veer
Straighten the log by veering & crossing the log perpendicular to the frame of the bike
Anticipatory Veer

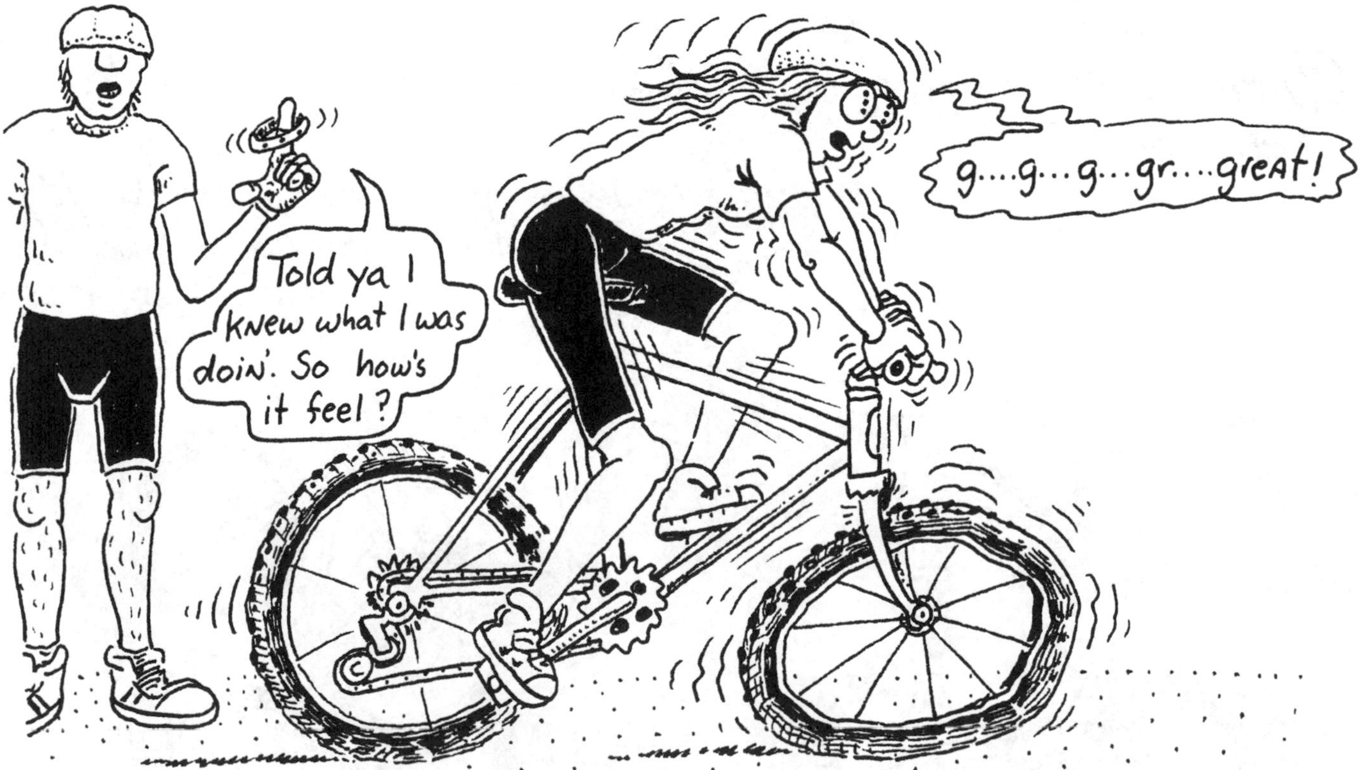
Told ya I knew what I was doin'. So how's it feel?
g…g…g…gr…great!

A spoke wrench is a dangerous tool in the hands of a neophyte…

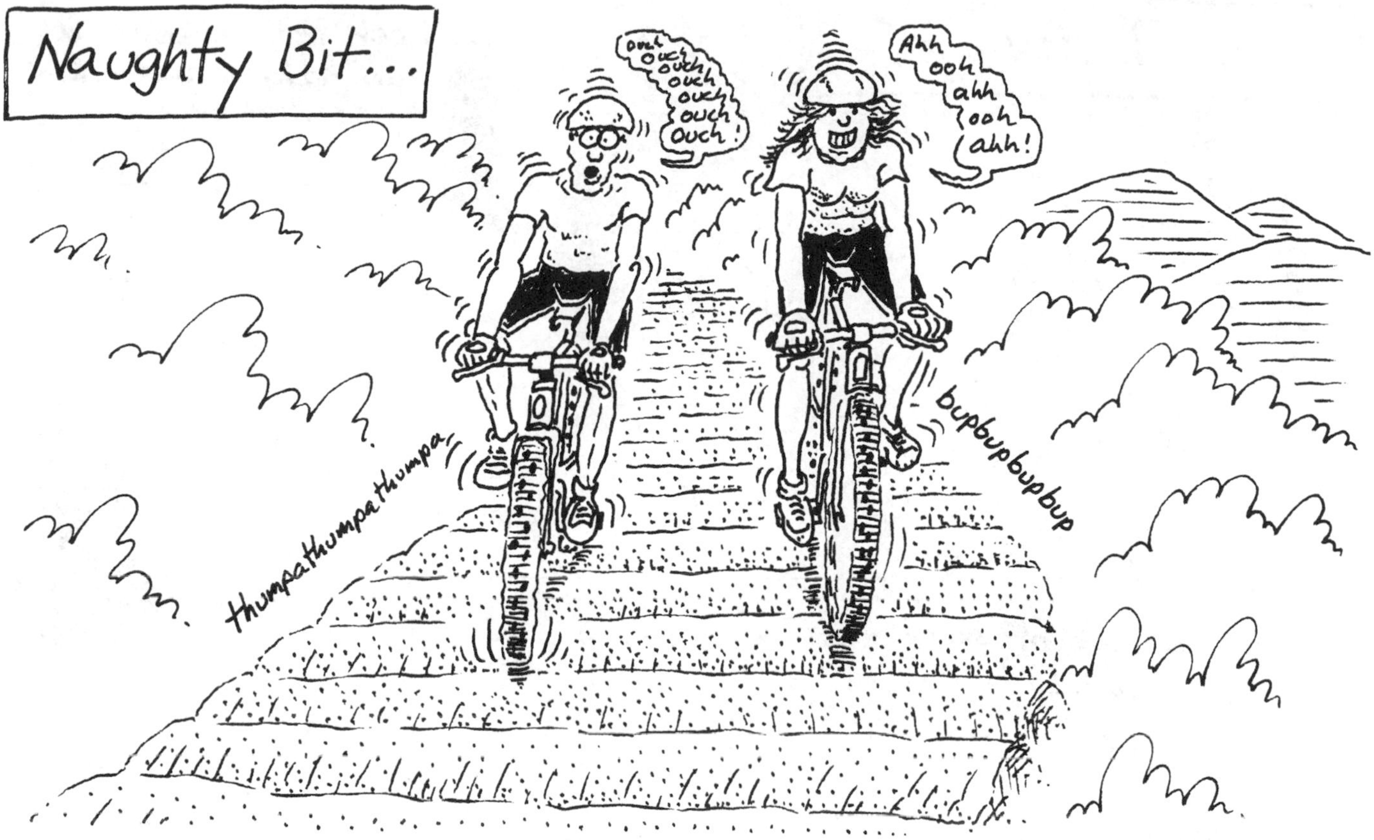
Naughty Bit...
ouch ouch ouch ouch ouch ouch Ouch!
Ahh ooh ahh ooh ahh!
thumpathumpathumpa
bupbupbupbup

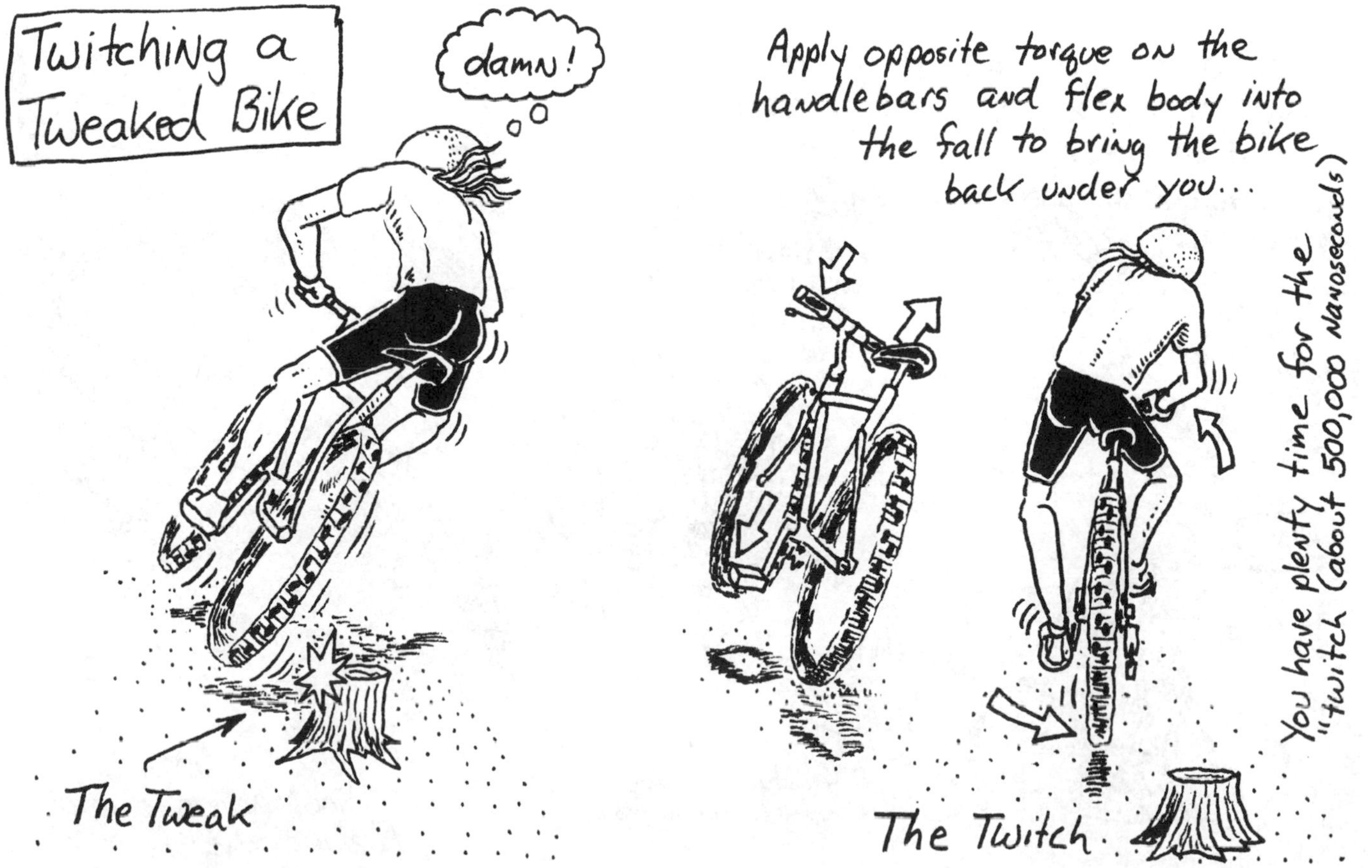
Twitching a Tweaked Bike
damn!
The Tweak
Apply opposite torque on the handlebars and flex body into the fall to bring the bike back under you...
You have plenty time for the "twitch (about 500,000 Nanoseconds)
The Twitch

# Steep Technique*

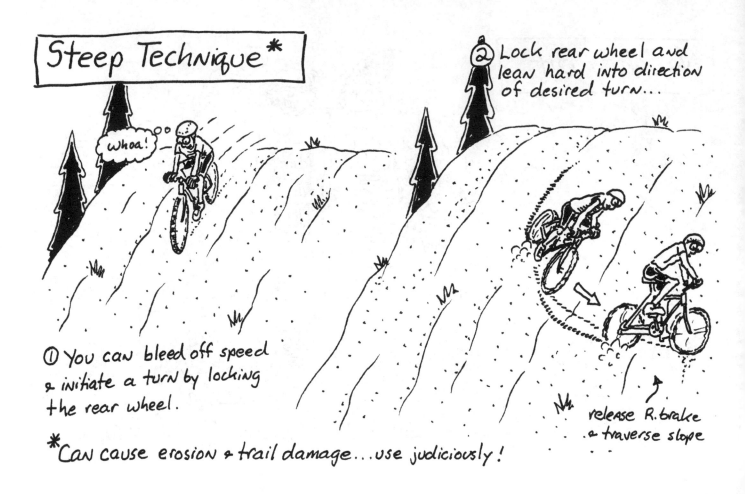

② Lock rear wheel and lean hard into direction of desired turn...

① You can bleed off speed & initiate a turn by locking the rear wheel.

*Can cause erosion & trail damage...use judiciously!

release R. brake & traverse slope

③ Now for the tricky part, reversing direction. The key to this move is to use a sideways front wheel as a brake...

lock rear wheel, cut front wheel & lean hard inside the turn...

Fall line

whew!

woosh!

front wheel almost perpendicular to frame

Aiiieee!

...without going over the handlebars.

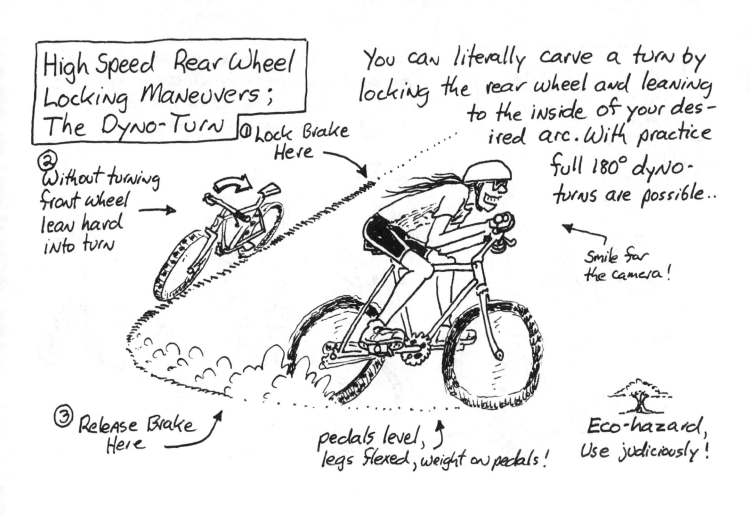

High Speed Rear Wheel Locking Maneuvers; The Dyno-Turn

You can literally carve a turn by locking the rear wheel and leaning to the inside of your desired arc. With practice full 180° dyno-turns are possible..

① Lock Brake Here

② Without turning front wheel lean hard into turn

③ Release Brake Here

Smile for the camera!

pedals level, legs flexed, weight on pedals!

Eco-hazard, Use judiciously!

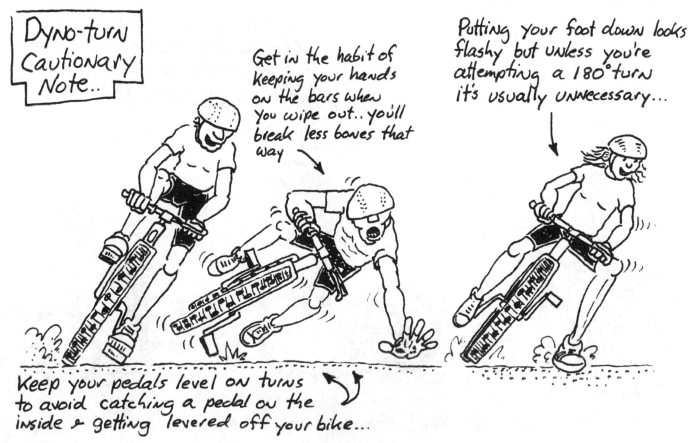

Dyno-turn Cautionary Note..

Get in the habit of keeping your hands on the bars when you wipe out.. you'll break less bones that way

Putting your foot down looks flashy but unless you're attempting a 180° turn it's usually unnecessary...

Keep your pedals level on turns to avoid catching a pedal on the inside & getting levered off your bike...

51

## The Dynamic Bar-hop

Warning! If you mess up and get tangled on the handlebars you'll do a dynamic face-dab. This is a low-speed desperation maneuver.

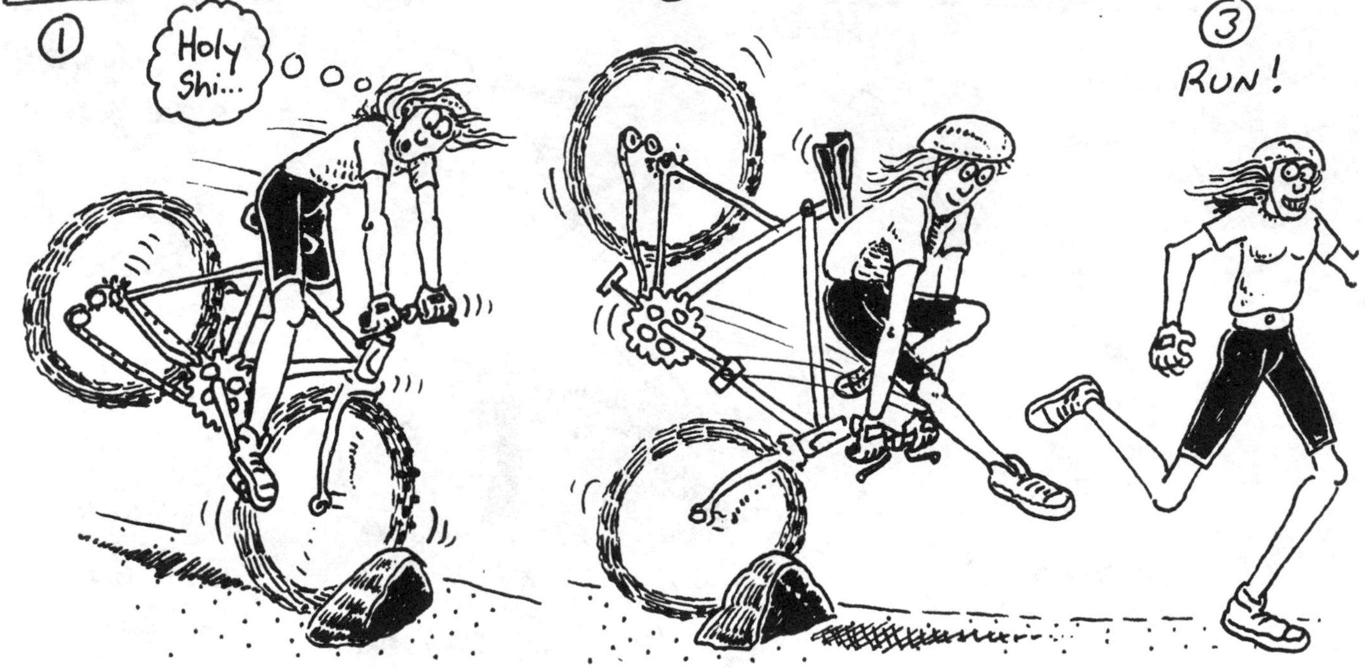

②
①
Holy Shi...
③
RUN!


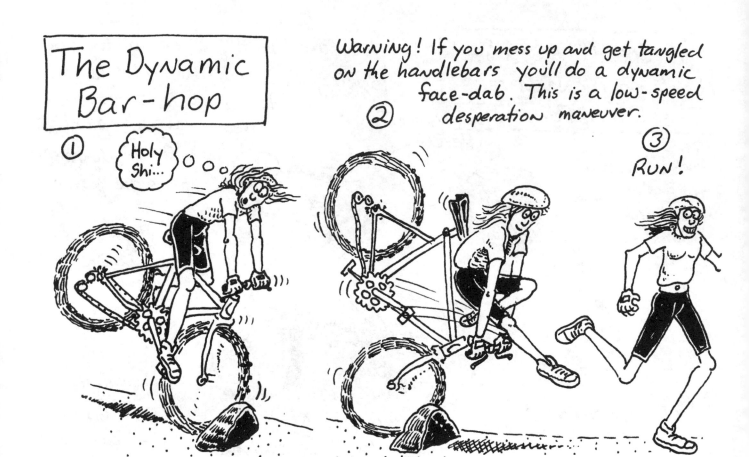

## Scootering a Crippled Bike..

If you break a chain way back in the boonies (or pretzel a derailleur, etc.) and lack the proper tools for a road repair don't push your bike, scooter it!

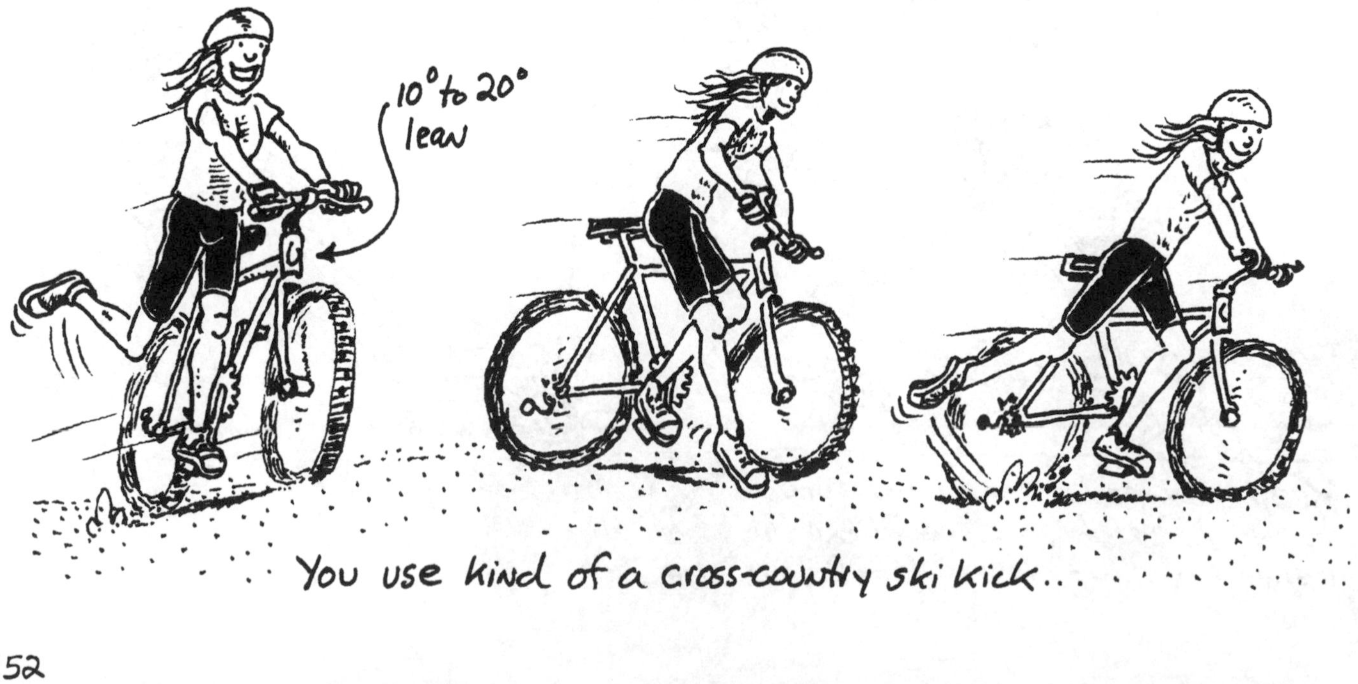

10° to 20° lean


You use kind of a cross-country ski kick..

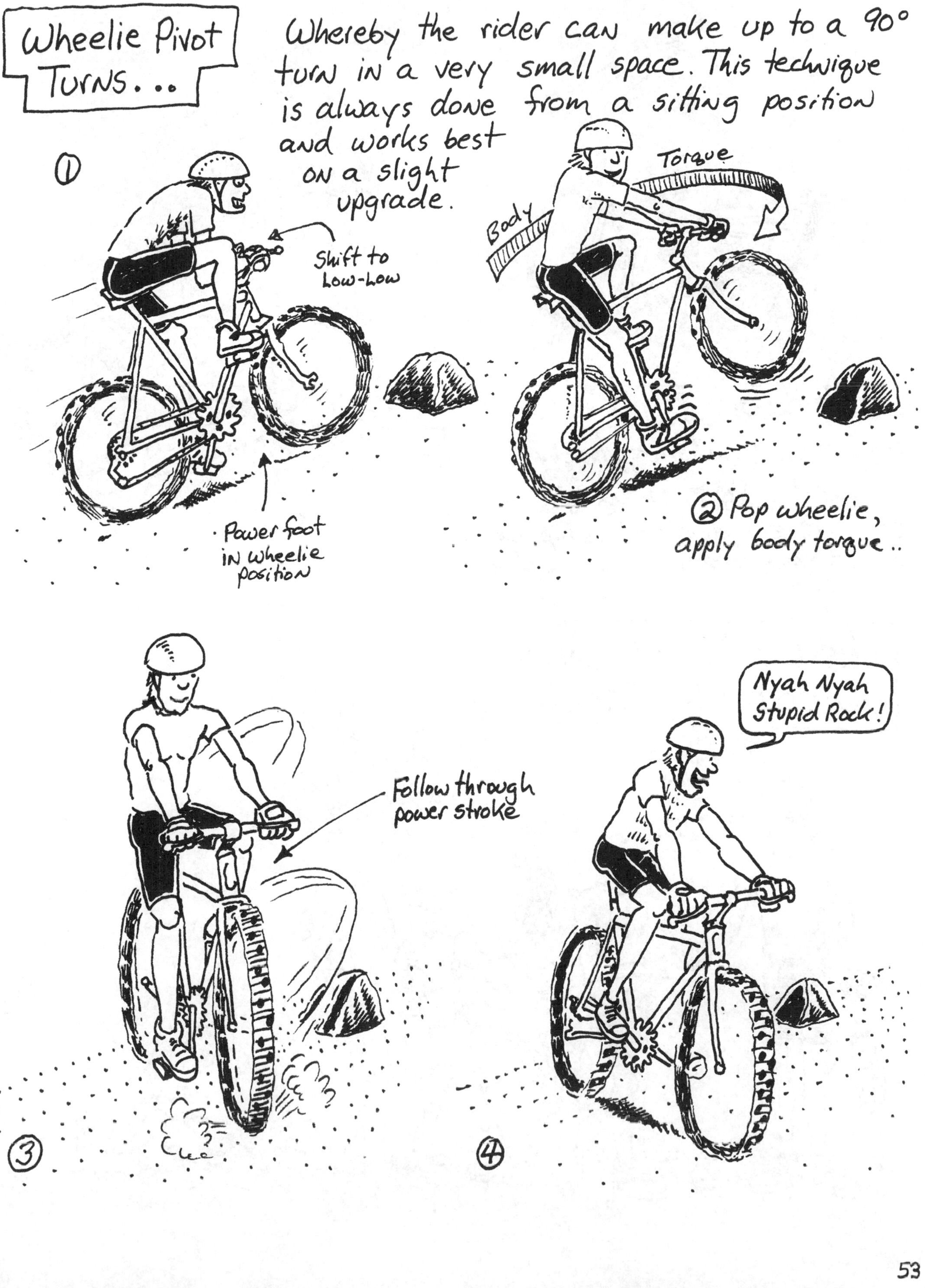
Wheelie Pivot Turns...
Whereby the rider can make up to a 90° turn in a very small space. This technique is always done from a sitting position and works best on a slight upgrade.
①
Shift to Low-Low
Power foot in wheelie position
Torque
Body
② Pop wheelie, apply body torque..
Follow through power stroke
③
Nyah Nyah Stupid Rock!
④

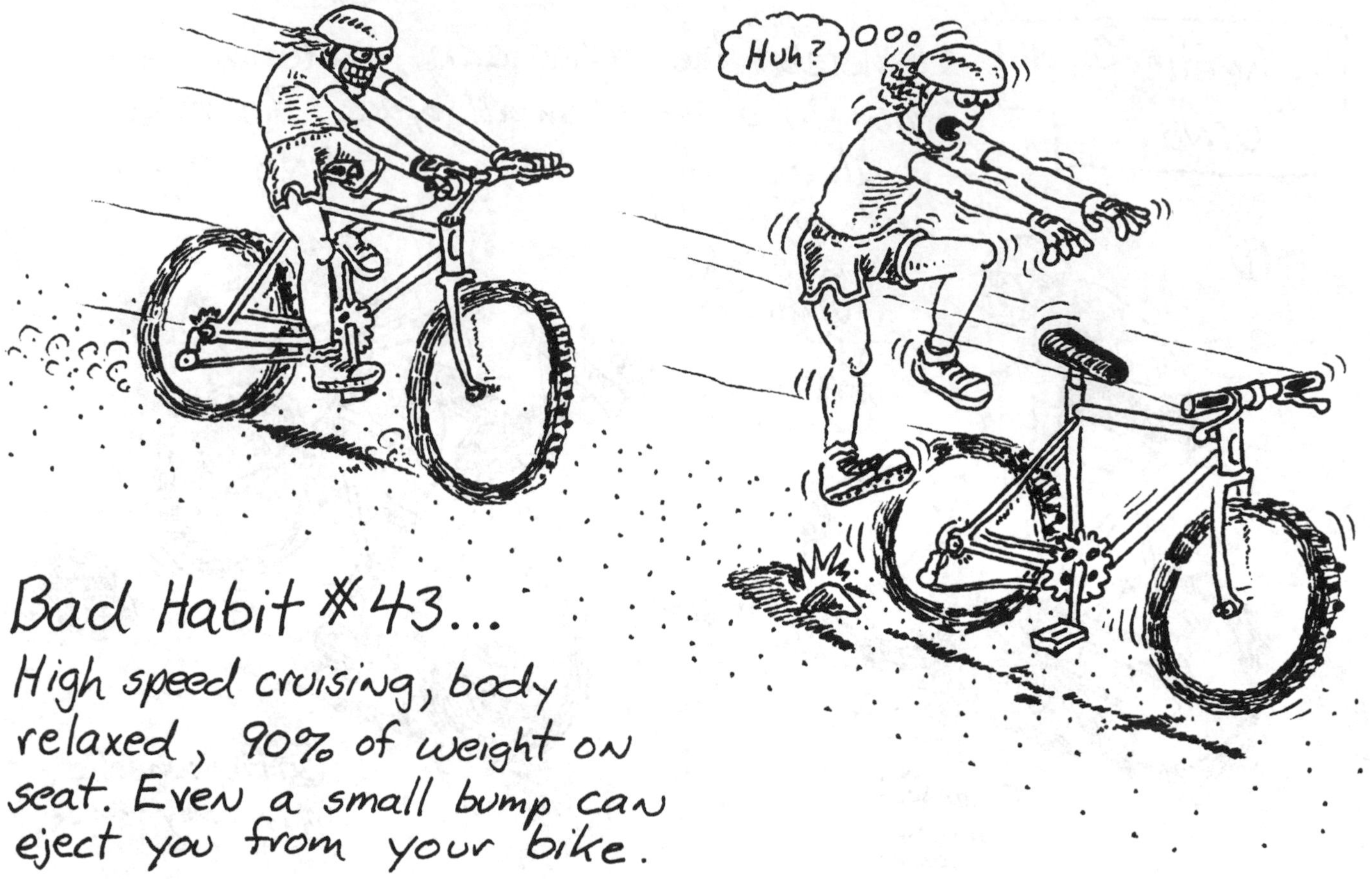
Huh?

Bad Habit #43...

High speed cruising, body relaxed, 90% of weight on seat. Even a small bump can eject you from your bike.

The Old "Tequila in the Water Bottle" Trick..

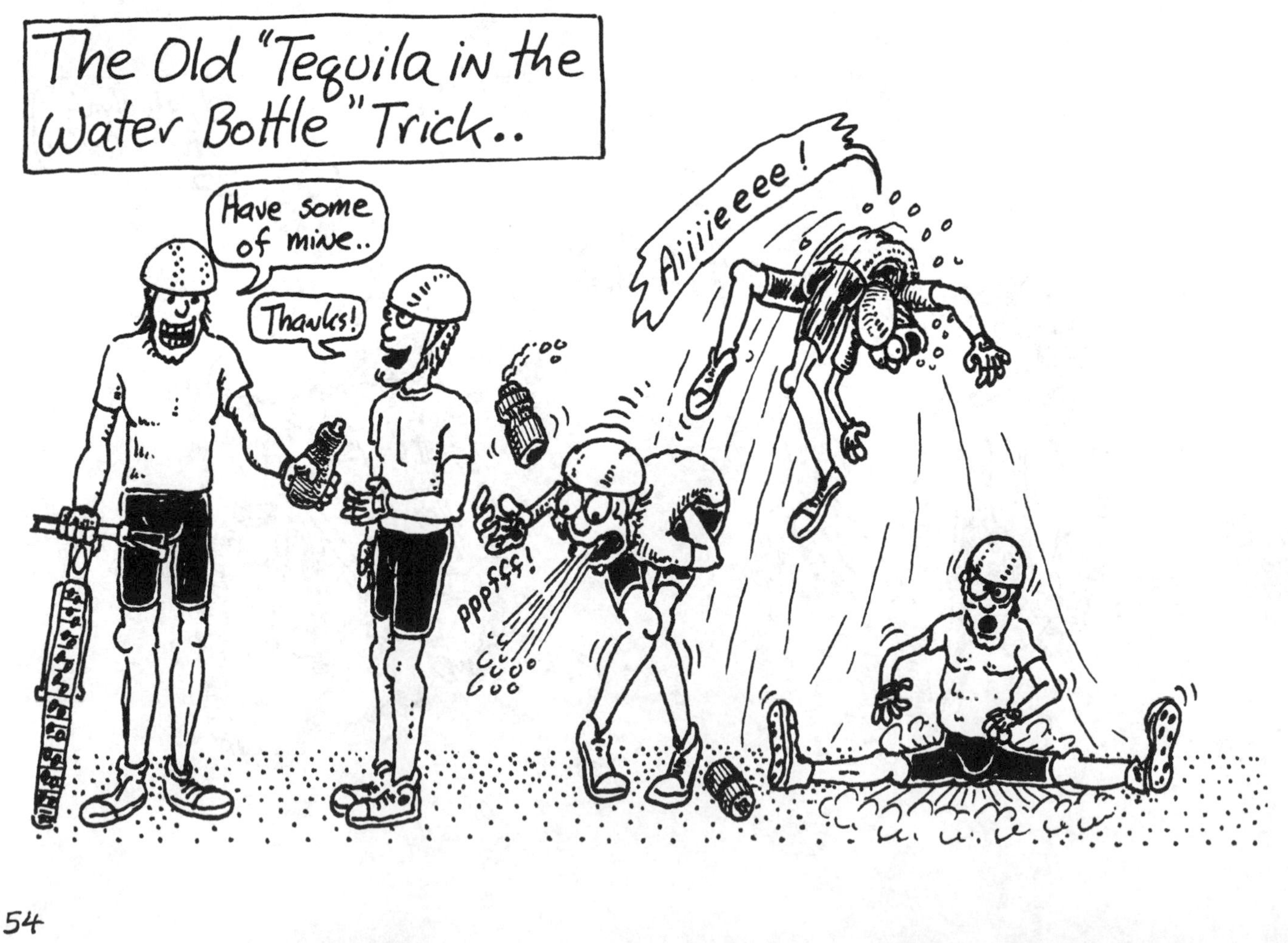
Have some of mine..
Thanks!
pppfff!
Aiiiieeee!

## Weighting the Rear Wheel

Whenever you make a sudden transition into sand, loose/deep gravel, or water get behind your seat to prevent loss of control.

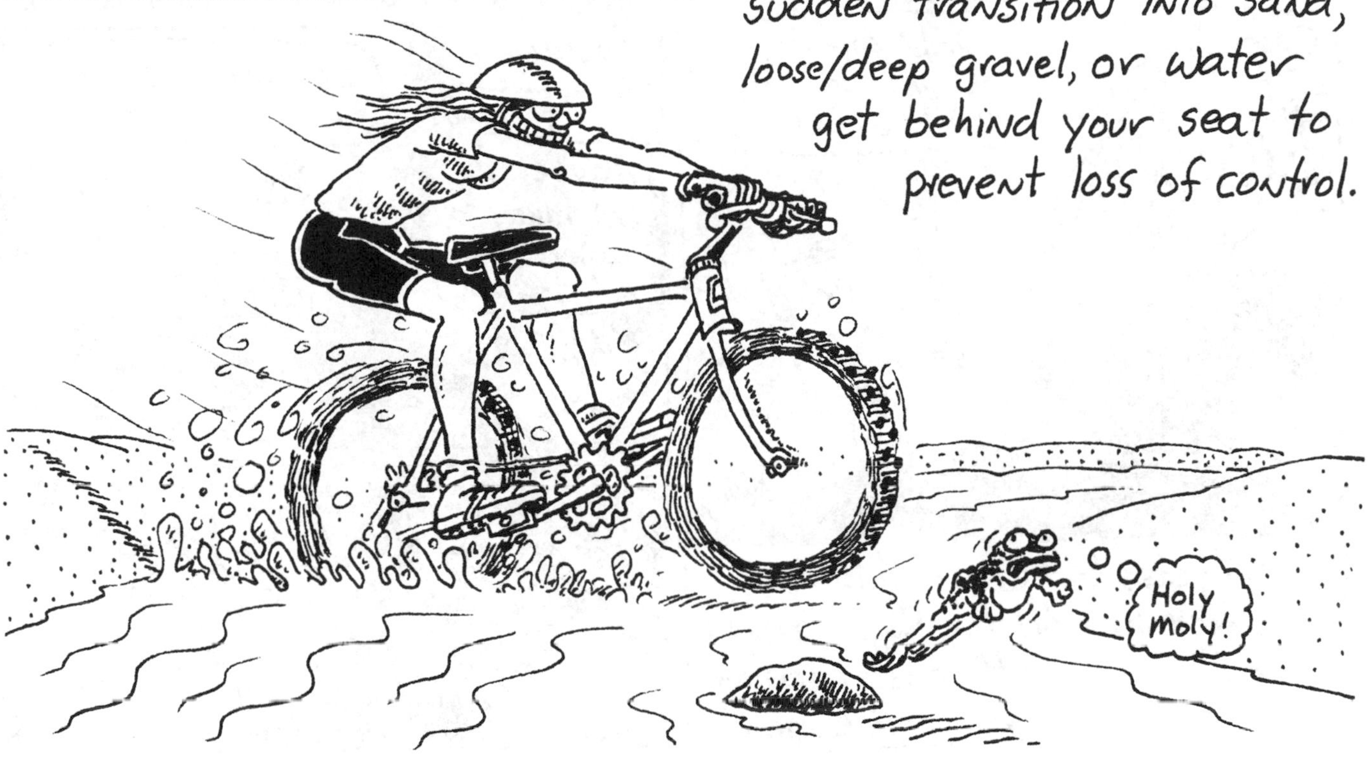
Holy moly!

## More Rear Wheel Weighting..

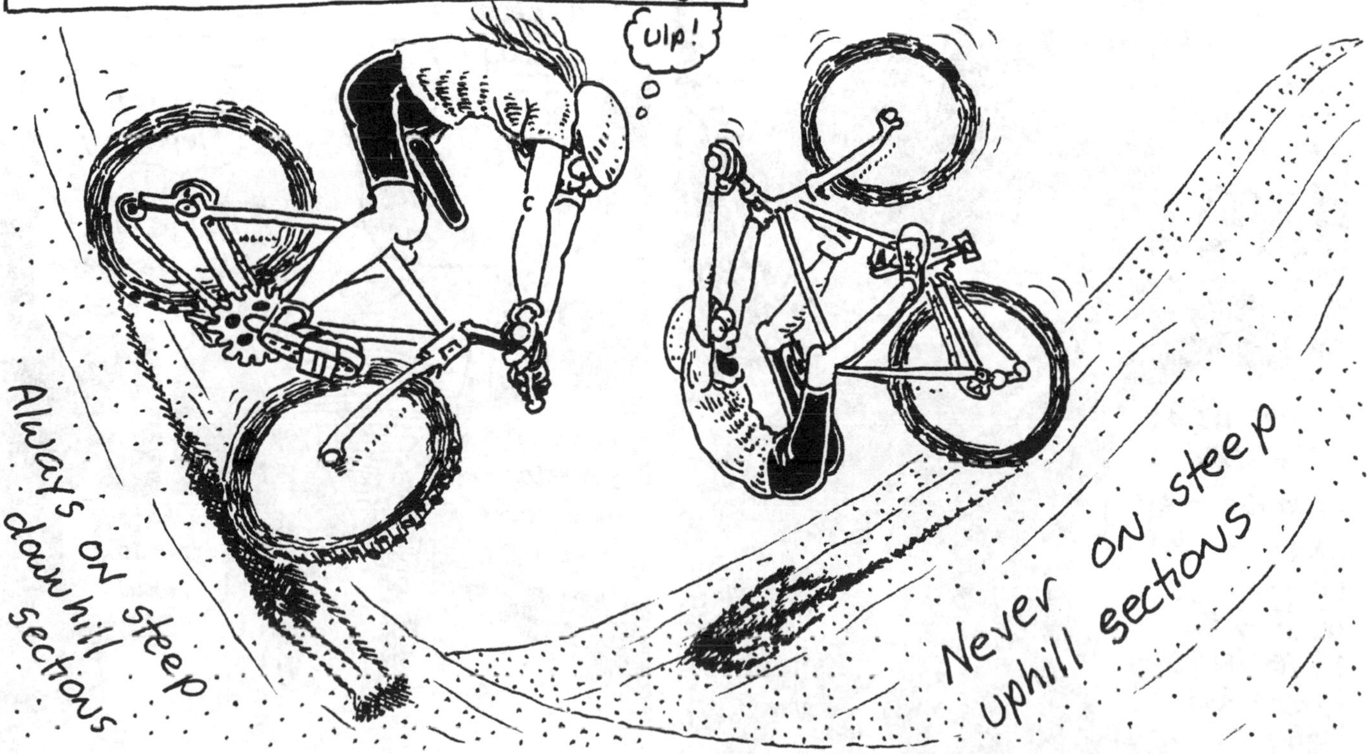
Ulp!
Always on steep downhill sections
Never on steep uphill sections

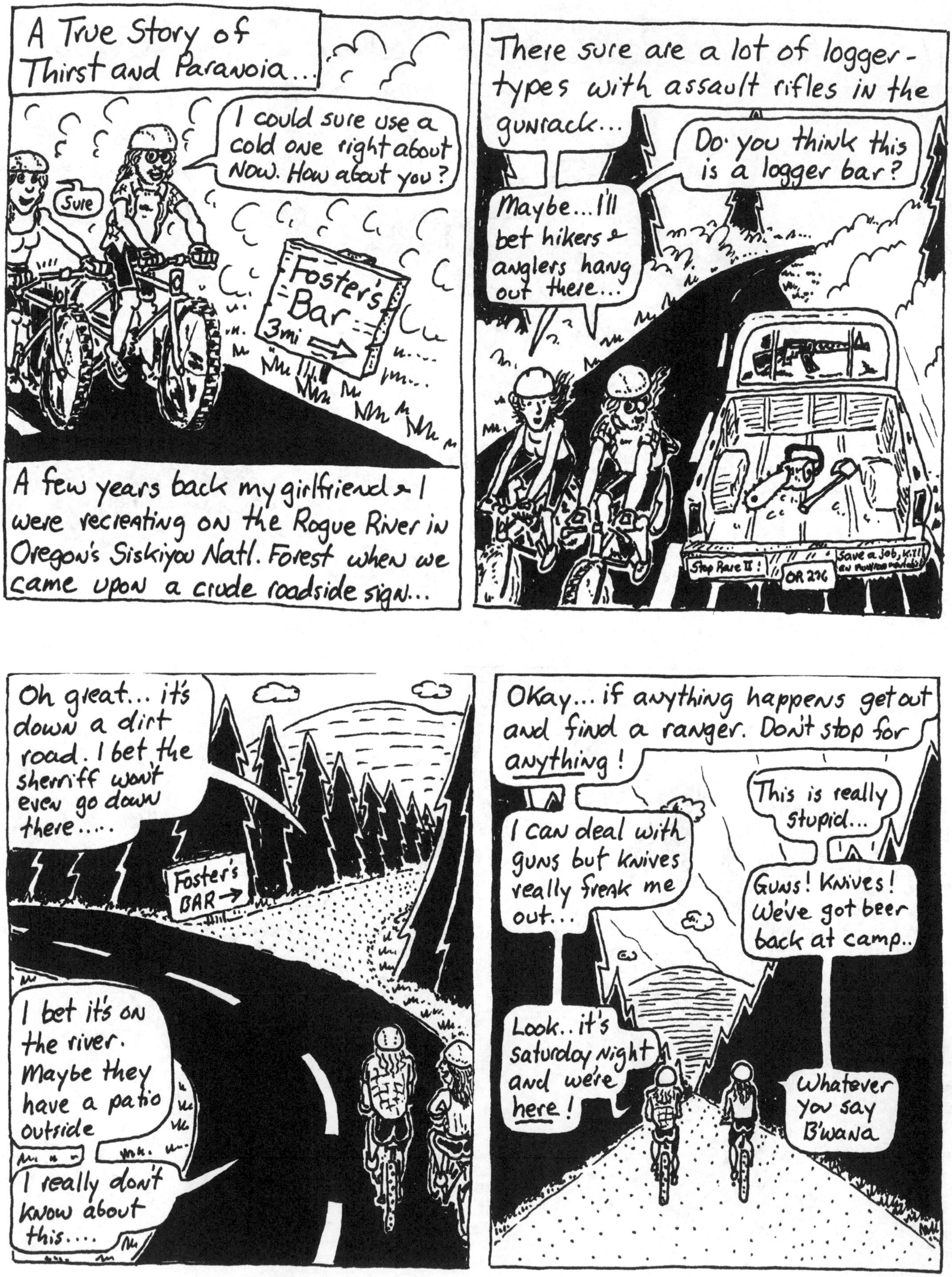
A True Story of Thirst and Paranoia...
I could sure use a cold one right about Now. How about you?
Sure
Foster's Bar 3mi
A few years back my girlfriend & I were recreating on the Rogue River in Oregon's Siskiyou Natl. Forest when we came upon a crude roadside sign...
There sure are a lot of logger-types with assault rifles in the gunrack...
Do you think this is a logger bar?
Maybe... I'll bet hikers & anglers hang out there...
Stop Rare II!
OR 276
Save a job, kill
Oh great... it's down a dirt road. I bet the sherriff won't even go down there....
Foster's BAR →
I bet it's on the river. Maybe they have a patio outside
I really don't know about this....
Okay... if anything happens get out and find a ranger. Don't stop for anything!
This is really stupid...
I can deal with guns but knives really freak me out...
Guns! Knives! We've got beer back at camp..
Look.. it's saturday night and we're here!
Whatever you say B'wana

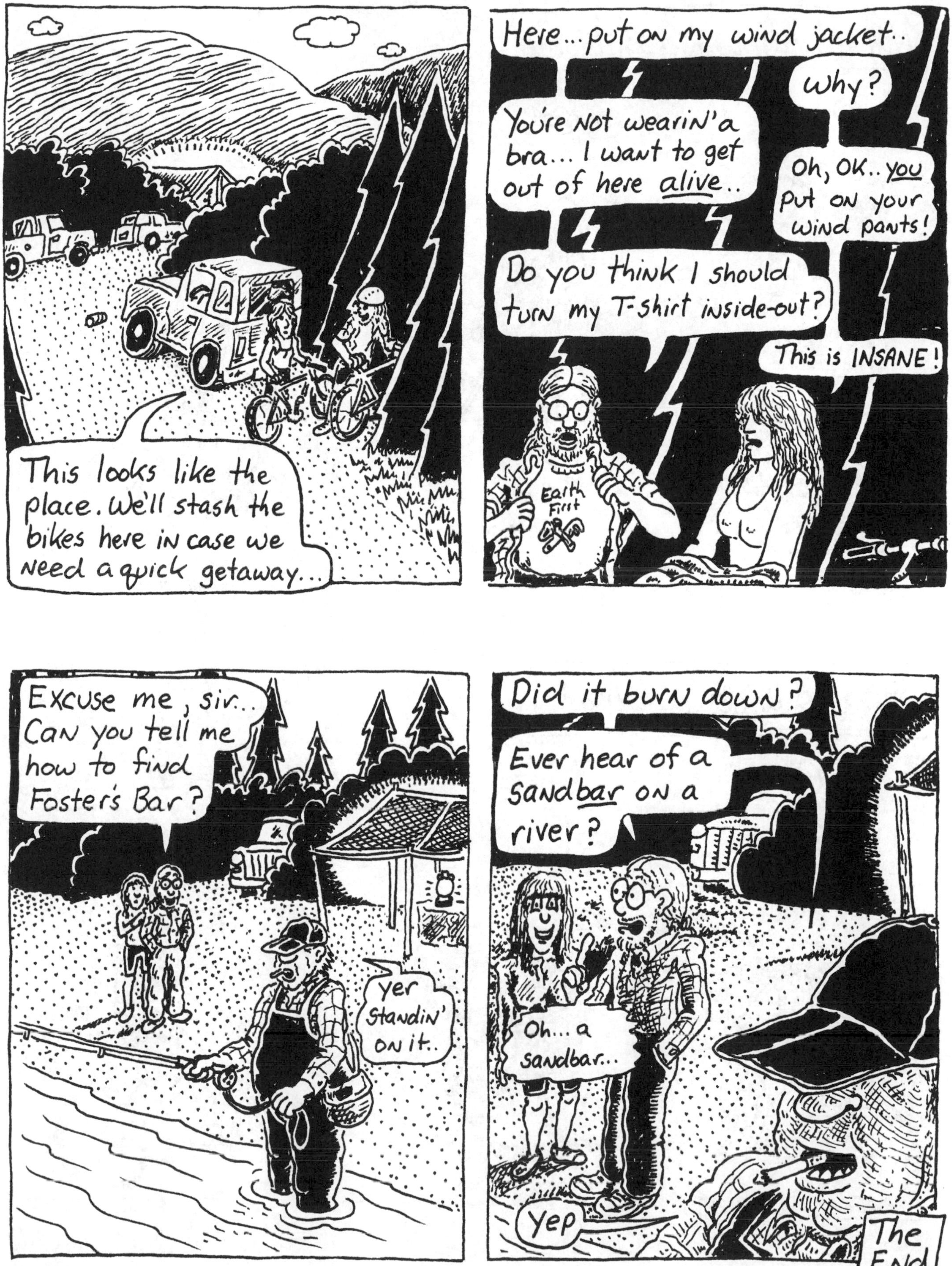
This looks like the place. We'll stash the bikes here in case we need a quick getaway...
Here... put on my wind jacket..
Why?
You're not wearin' a bra... I want to get out of here alive..
Oh, OK.. you put on your wind pants!
Do you think I should turn my T-shirt inside-out?
This is INSANE!
Earth First
Excuse me, sir.. Can you tell me how to find Foster's Bar?
yer standin' on it..
Did it burn down?
Ever hear of a sandbar on a river?
Oh... a sandbar..
Yep
The End

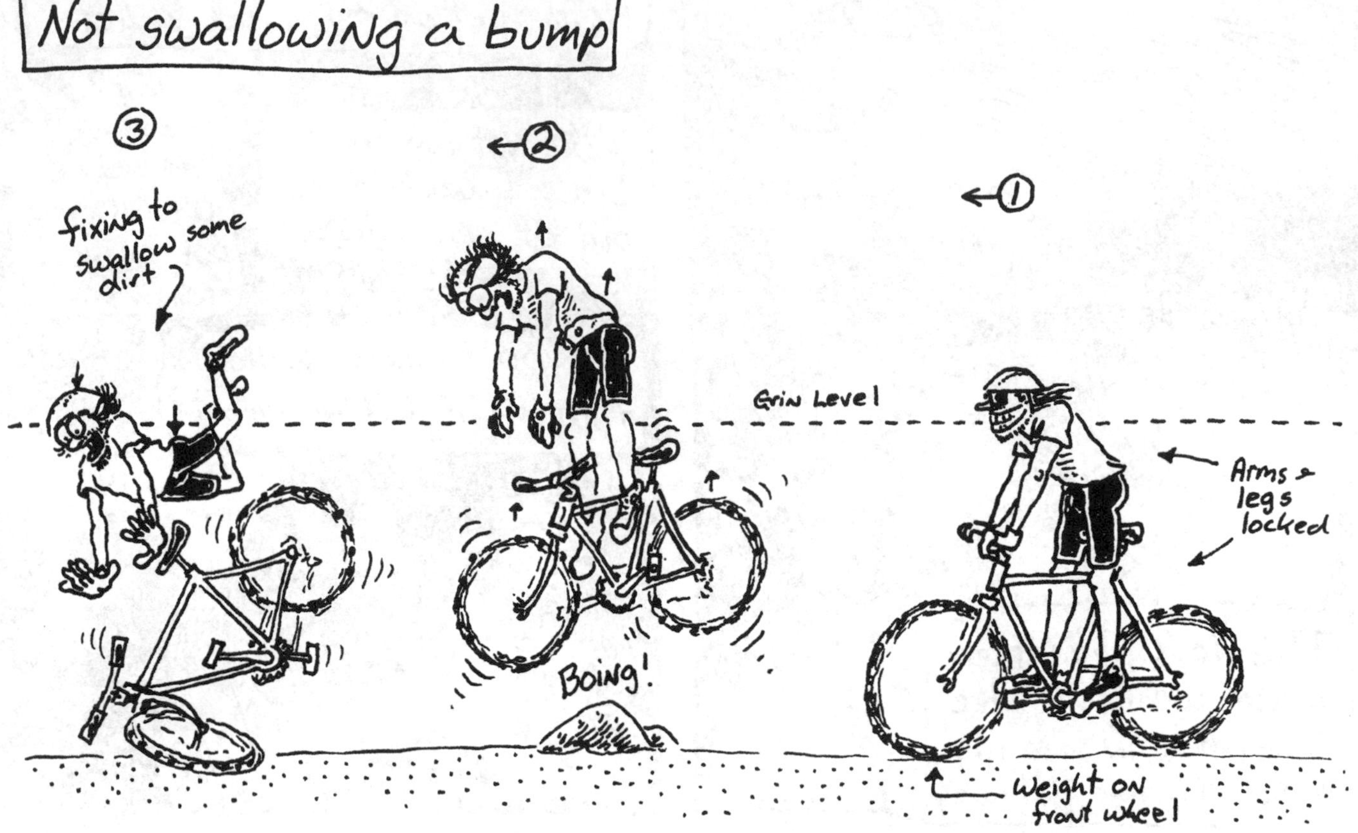
Not swallowing a bump
③
←②
←①
fixing to swallow some dirt
Grin Level
Arms & legs locked
Boing!
Weight on front wheel

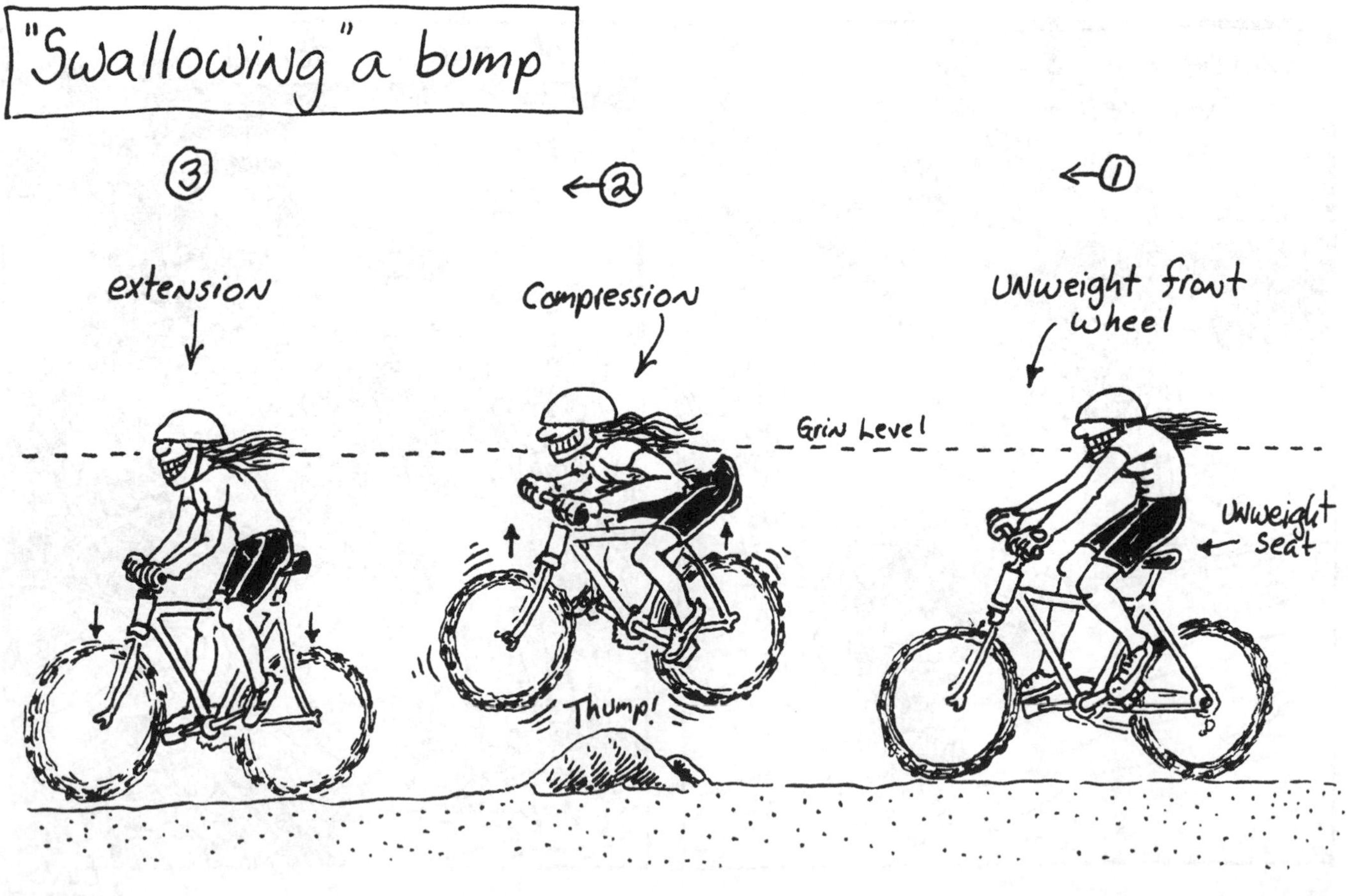
"Swallowing" a bump
③
←②
←①
extension
Compression
Unweight front wheel
Grin Level
Unweight seat
Thump!

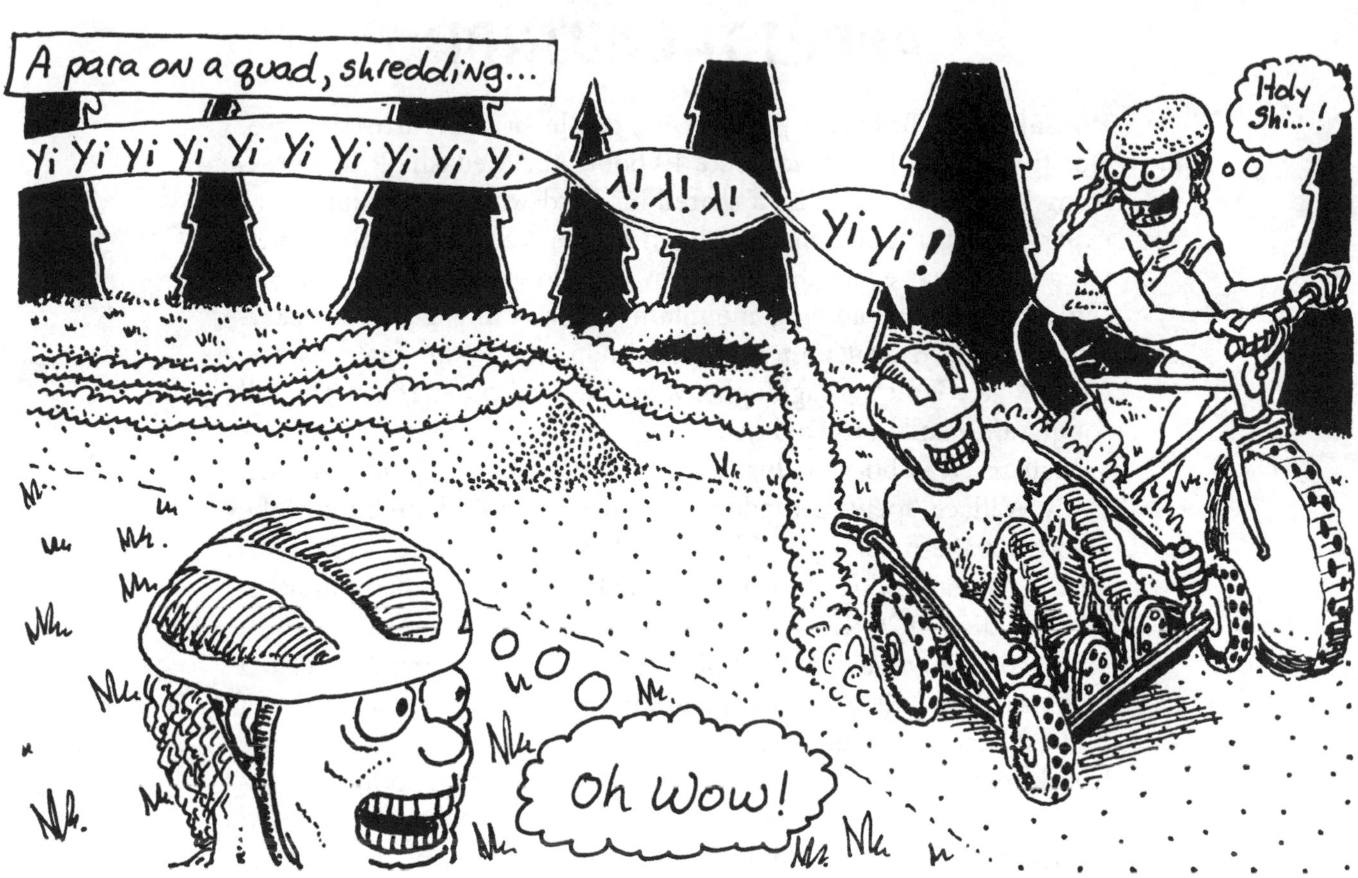
A para on a quad, shredding...
Yi Yi Yi Yi Yi Yi Yi Yi Yi Yi
Yi! Yi! Yi!
Yi Yi!
Holy Shi...!
Oh Wow!

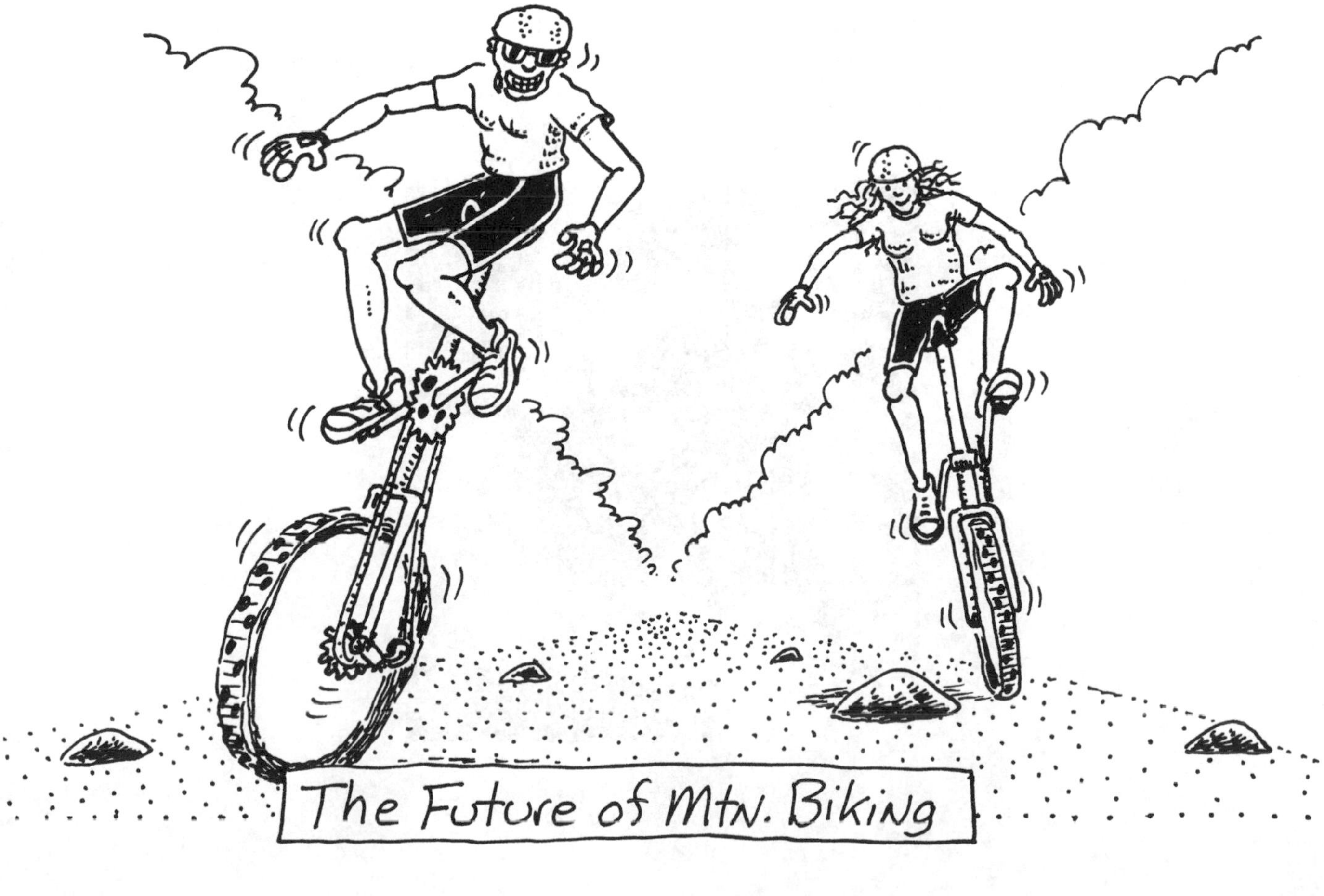

The Future of Mtn. Biking

# ABOUT THE AUTHOR

**William "Not Bill" Nealy** was a wild, gentle, brilliant artist and creator turned cult hero who wrote 10 books for Menasha Ridge Press from 1982 to 2000. William shared his hard-won "crash-and-learn" experiences through humorous hand-drawn cartoons and illustrated river maps that enabled generations to follow in his footsteps. His subjects included paddling, mountain biking, skiing, and inline skating. His hand-drawn, poster-size river maps of the Nantahala, Ocoee, Chattooga, Gauley, Youghiogheny, and several other rivers are still sought after and in use today.

William was born in Birmingham, Alabama. He and his wife, Holly Wallace, spent their adult years in a home William built in the woods on the outskirts of Chapel Hill, North Carolina, along with an assortment of dogs, lizards, pigs, snakes, turtles, and amphibians. William died in 2001.

His longtime friend and publisher, Bob Sehlinger, wrote: "When William Nealy died in 2001, paddling lost its poet laureate, one of its best teachers, and its greatest icon. William was arguably the best-known ambassador of whitewater sport, entertaining and instructing hundreds of thousands of paddlers through his illustrated books, including the classics: *Whitewater Home Companion Volumes I and II, Whitewater Tales of Terror, Kayaks to Hell,* and his best-known work, *Kayak,* which combined expert paddling instruction with artful caricatures and parodies of the whitewater community itself."

You can learn more about William, his art, and his many books at thewilliamnealy.com.

photo: MAGPIE

Printed in the USA
CPSIA information can be obtained
at www.ICGtesting.com
JSHW061121250823
47224JS00002B/5

9 781634 043687